Second Nature

Second Nature

HOW TO BUILD ECOHABITS THAT STICK

Lori Downs

Oxford Comma Press LLC
Metairie, LA

Copyright © 2026 by Lori Downs

All rights reserved.

No part of this book may be used to train artificial intelligence (AI) systems or technologies without express written permission from the copyright holder.

The information in this book is for educational purposes only and does not constitute professional advice. The author and publisher disclaim any liability arising from its use.

The author has no responsibility for the persistence or accuracy of URLs for external or third-party Internet websites referred to in this publication and does not guarantee that any content on such websites is, or will remain, accurate or appropriate.

All trademarks and brand names mentioned in this book are the property of their respective owners.

Cover design by Lori Downs. Cover illustration ©PassakornProthein, used under license via Canva.com.

Second Nature: How to Build Ecohabits That Stick / Lori Downs, First Edition
Library of Congress Control Number: 2026900922
ISBN: 979-8-9939387-0-7 (Paperback)
979-8-9939387-1-4 (E-book)

Published 2026 by Oxford Comma Press LLC
oxfordcommapress.com

Printed in the United States of America

For Caleb and Sarah
You inspire me to do better every single day
and
In memory of Dakota Stormer
Your legacy still lights the way

*Coming together is a beginning;
keeping together is progress;
working together is success.*

–EDWARD EVERETT HALE

Contents

You Can Change the World 1

Understand Why 7

Why Save Earth? 9

Why Aren't We Doing More to Save Earth? 19

Create Habits That Stick 25

The Anatomy of a Habit 27

Get Ready 35

Put Your Ecohabit Together 43

Ideas to Get You Started 53

Anticipate and Overcome Obstacles 77

Define Success 81

Get Going! 85

Break Bad Habits 93

Increase Your Impact 99

Cultivate Your Ecohabits 101

Inspire Others to Do Better 105

Move Outside of Your Inner Circle 109

Enjoy the Results of Your Hard Work 117

Habit Building Worksheets 119

Other Ways to Live More Sustainably 127

References 135

Author's Note 141

Acknowledgments 143

INTRODUCTION

You Can Change the World

Well, not by yourself, but you have a part to play! Making positive environmental changes to the world is not the responsibility of certain groups of people, governments, or companies alone. Every one of us has the responsibility to reflect on our behavior and its impact and determine how we can do better. We cannot sit back and wait–we must create change–starting now.

Why now?

Humans are causing a dangerous decline in nature, according to the United Nations Environment Program:

- Human activities have significantly changed three-quarters of Earth's land surface.
- Almost 90% of Earth's marine stocks are fully exploited, over-exploited, or depleted.
- Human activities have pushed one million species of plants and animals to extinction.

- Society's current way of life is using more of the Earth's natural resources than our ecosystems can keep up with.

You might feel like your actions are small and inconsequential, so maybe you put little effort or thought into contributing. Perhaps you made eco-friendly changes for a little while but later fell off the wagon. Maybe you felt it was too overwhelming and got discouraged.

Books, websites, blogs, and social media pages tell us what to do to be more eco-friendly. I follow some of them, and maybe you do too. They say things like, "Use this!" (and buy it from them) or "Do that!" but they leave out how to cement those tools and actions into our lives, so they last. I should stop using plastic straws and not set the thermostat too high in the winter, using excess energy. I need to remember to take our reusable bags to the store and to recycle. That's fine, but recycling didn't magically happen at my house once I set up a new bin.

We recycled for a few days or weeks. Then we moved the bin, or we got lazy and started tossing everything into the trashcan when the recycling bin got full. I'd hazard to guess you have failed at least once (maybe more often!) at trying to make new environmentally friendly changes stick. Yet you keep returning to the idea of living more sustainably and want to try again.

Does this describe you?

If you're holding this book, you've already decided you want to work on living sustainably to protect our planet and improve the quality of life for future generations. You're aware our environment needs help, and you're willing to change how you live to make an impact. Or maybe you've already tweaked your behavior and lifestyle to be eco-friendly but want to augment your efforts. *Second Nature* aims to help you do all of that.

What if I told you I can help make your eco-friendly changes stick?

This book will teach you to create positive, helpful habits that stick. I won't just share what to do to live sustainably and leave you on your own. I'll help you step by step to turn those changes into long-lasting ecohabits. **You'll learn:**

- Reasons we should live sustainably as a global society and why we aren't living as sustainably as we could
- The anatomy of habits and how they work
- How to create a new habit or change one that isn't so environmentally friendly
- How to build upon your new ecohabit successes to help others build their own new ecohabits

We tend to forget that when combined, we compound the effect of the changes we make. Don't underestimate the fact that others are making small changes like you. If we all wait for someone else to take the first action, we won't progress. Imagine the impact we can make if billions of people genuinely believe their actions leave a mark.

By changing our behavior and making environmentally friendly choices, we're also setting an example for our friends, family, and–most importantly–our grandchildren. When others watch us choose a better planet, they will too.

Why should you listen to me?

I have dedicated myself to protecting our planet for more than 25 years. As a licensed environmental engineer in the energy industry, I've seen the havoc that a 200 million gallon oil spill can wreak on water, land, and wildlife. I understand the impact on air quality and our health that harmful emissions can bring. I know climate change is real, and we have a relatively short time frame to do something about it.

Every day, I strive to prevent catastrophes from happening and to design and implement new ways to reduce and eliminate my company's and our customers' negative impacts on the environment. The changes we make aren't "one and done." They are cultural changes embedded in our behavior and ways of working. The underlying principles of habit change (like consistency and clear triggers) apply at a global corporation, in a household, or for an individual. Building habits takes time and will meet resistance no matter the setting before they become automatic.

My family and I have successfully implemented many ecohabits throughout the years, by changing our behaviors (meal planning and cooking from the pantry to reduce food waste) and the products we use (reusable versus disposable napkins). You'll hear about some of these throughout this book. I hope they motivate you!

Why us?

Many governments and businesses around the world are aiming to improve their environmental footprint because society expects them to do better. Argentina and Costa Rica have initiatives to protect forests and national parks. The Coca-Cola Company is on a mission to reduce virgin, oil-based plastic in its bottles and has unveiled a beverage bottle made from 100% plant-based plastic.

But are each of us also improving as individual members of the global society? If we expect companies and governments to be held accountable, we must hold ourselves accountable too. If I can help a multinational company change its behavior and get those changes to stick, I can help you get your behavior changes to stick too.

You might be thinking right now, "Do I have what it takes to adjust my behavior?" "How do I even start?" "Will I be able to keep it up after I make a change? I've tried before and failed." You may not think you have the power or motivation to make a difference.

I'm here to tell you that you do.

No matter your second guesses, no matter what people tell you. You wouldn't have picked up this book if you didn't, and I believe in you. Think about how you'll feel when you've made a lasting change! Caring for our Earth is a form of self-care. The healthier our planet, the healthier we become.

Whether your home is big or small, regardless of your age or occupation, opportunities to live sustainably exist for anyone willing to make a change. Once you've built your first ecohabit, you'll feel your world brighten knowing you contributed to a healthier planet. You'll want to make another change. You'll get hooked on making a difference.

Turn the page, and let's shape the one small change that will start it all!

PART ONE

Understand Why

We rarely jump into changing our lives without a compelling reason to do so. You don't find a new job unless there's a powerful driver to leave your old one: poor working conditions, insufficient salary, or it's too far from home, and the like. You don't start eating healthily for no reason. Maybe you have a medical condition requiring you to cut back on certain foods to control your blood levels before things worsen. The same applies to improving our environmental impact. **Why should we change?**

The information in this part of *Sec2ond Nature* may be new to you or reiterate what you already know. Either way, it lays the groundwork for the rest of the book, so don't let it put you off if you already believe your habits need to change. You can also use Part 1 to help convince the skeptics in your life that the Earth needs us to change. It's full of talking points and data to help you frame those conversations.

Part 1 covers reasons for
- Conserving and protecting water

- Conserving energy
- Reducing waste
- Living sustainably

It also investigates several reasons we aren't moving faster, such as

- We don't think it's our responsibility.
- We don't see the urgency.
- We think our actions won't have a meaningful impact.
- We think it costs too much time and money.

CHAPTER 1

Why Save Earth?

> A true conservationist is a man who knows that the world is not given by his fathers but borrowed from his children.
>
> – JOHN JAMES AUDUBON

Our planet faces significant challenges, but there is hope for recovery. We are at a pivotal point in improving the health of our planet. While humanity is the greatest threat to Earth, we still have the chance to save our planet from complete irreversible destruction. Earth has shown repeatedly that it can heal if we help. My hometown of New Orleans sits along the shores of Lake Pontchartrain, the second largest inland saltwater body in the United States. The lake is a vital resource for economic development, recreation, and sustainability, not only for New Orleans but for Louisiana. For years, polluted Lake Pontchartrain suffered from shell dredging and urban runoff of sewage and chemicals. After decades of challenging work through partnerships with federal and local governmental agencies and non-governmental organizations, the lake is a much cleaner, healthier body of water.

It is often difficult to understand the total environmental footprint of a product or activity, but **living sustainably depends on focusing on three key areas: water use, energy use, and waste generation**. You can probably think of other things that are important to preserving our natural habitat, but these three are big ones that touch all the others. They are areas we all recognize and impact through our daily habits. We don't need to wait for governments, corporations, or society to change our personal behavior. Nor should we!

Why conserve and protect water?

Water covers almost three-quarters of the Earth's surface. That must mean it's essentially an unlimited resource, right? Wrong. Less than 1% of Earth's surface water is usable. The United States Geological Survey reports that nearly all the water on Earth's surface is saltwater held in our oceans. This water is too salty for us to use without treatment. Ice and glaciers tie up over two-thirds of the world's clean fresh water. Groundwater comprises about a third of our fresh water. Most communities use freshwater provided by rivers, but this water is only one ten-thousandth of a percent (0.0001%) of the water on Earth. That's hardly any! It may not seem like it, but most of the world's freshwater is not accessible to us, and what is accessible is becoming less so in many areas.

Britannica defines water scarcity as "insufficient freshwater resources to meet the human and environmental demands of an area." Two types of water scarcity exist. **Physical water scarcity** is not having enough water available to meet the needs of an area. This type of scarcity occurs in arid or semi-arid regions and can sometimes be seasonal. The Colorado River basin is an example of physical water scarcity. The river is a vital resource for about 40 million people from Denver to Los Angeles. Its reservoirs have been declining toward critically low levels after years of dry conditions and increased temperatures.

Insufficient or nonexistent infrastructure to deliver water to an area results in **economic water scarcity**. Sufficient water volumes may be available, but accessibility is a problem. An example of economic water scarcity exists in Mexico City, where over 20 million people live. Although the region receives adequate rainfall each year, most of the water becomes contaminated runoff into the sewer system because of the urban nature of the city. Little rainfall makes its way to replenish the local aquifers that feed nearly half the municipal supply. Mexico City regularly experiences water shortages and is one of the top cities in the world threatened by water scarcity.

Not only is water scarcity an issue, but water use has grown at twice the rate of the population in the last century. Over 2 billion people lack safely managed drinking water, over 3 billion lack basic hand washing facilities at home, and water scarcity could displace 700 million people from where they live by 2030, according to the United Nations.

There are many reasons to conserve water and protect its quality—we need water for almost everything we do. This resource is essential for producing food, clothing, electronics, energy, and more. We need water to bathe, cook, clean, and drink. Many of us enjoy our natural waterways and water bodies for recreation too. We must learn how to change our water use habits to conserve freshwater and ensure enough supplies for future use.

Why conserve energy?

As our world progresses, developing economies grow, technology booms, and the global population rises. However, this development leads to higher energy demand. Today, fossil fuels such as coal, oil, and natural gas primarily produce the energy needed to power and heat our planet. The challenge with fossil fuels is that when we burn them to generate energy, they produce greenhouse gases, among other pollutants.

These greenhouse gases (or GHGs) trap heat in Earth's atmosphere. In moderate amounts, GHGs are a good thing because they help keep heat from escaping back into space, making Earth warm enough for life to survive. However, the more these gases increase in the atmosphere, the more Earth's temperature rises. The amount of GHGs currently in the atmosphere is at a record high since the Industrial Revolution. We are experiencing never before seen global temperatures, resulting in climate change.

Climate change involves shifting weather patterns, including increased or decreased rain or snow, higher or lower temperatures, more intense hurricanes or typhoons, and rising water levels in some areas due to melting snow and ice. These changing weather patterns impact Earth negatively. Excessive cold and heat can threaten food production and impact public health. Heat and droughts increase plant and animal extinctions. Swinging weather patterns can raise the risk of extreme flooding and wildfires and even erode our coastlines.

Reducing GHGs won't happen overnight, just as the amount of GHGs in the atmosphere didn't increase overnight to get us to where we are today. Removing GHGs from the atmosphere will take decades. Significant GHG reductions will need governmental policies and regulation due to the challenge's size and severity.

We don't have to wait for governments, however. We can use energy wisely as we go about our day. Decreasing our energy use leaves more resources for future generations, reduces the demand placed on over-stressed energy systems, and saves us money today. We can even take advantage of renewable energy options like solar and wind if they are available. Depending on where we live, we can make greener transportation choices. And even more, we can talk to others–start a climate conversation to encourage them to consider how they use energy.

Why reduce waste?

Humans generate over 2 billion tons of trash annually. That's the same weight as 12 million blue whales–the heaviest animal in the world! By 2050, global waste volumes are expected to double the expected population growth. Experts predict that a third of the trash produced isn't managed in an environmentally safe manner.

Estimates show that globally we dispose of about half of our waste in a landfill, via recycling, or by composting. We burn twenty percent in incinerators and openly dump the rest. Dumped waste ends up in waterways and on beaches and impacts wildlife and their habitats. How often have you driven or walked through where you live and not seen trash on the ground? (If you live somewhere this is not commonplace, please let me know!) Plastic straws and bottles, aluminum cans, and grocery sacks are everywhere. We've all seen photos of sea turtles with plastic drink can holders embedded in their shells. I read that the ocean now contains one ton of plastic for every three tons of fish swimming around. That's like a Honda Civic's worth of plastic for an African elephant's weight in fish!

Even waste that is responsibly managed via incineration or landfilling can cause an environmental impact if the waste gas is not collected. Just like burning fuel, burning waste produces not only GHGs but releases toxic pollutants from the plastics, metals, and materials burned. Organic materials decomposing in landfills also naturally release methane and other GHGs.

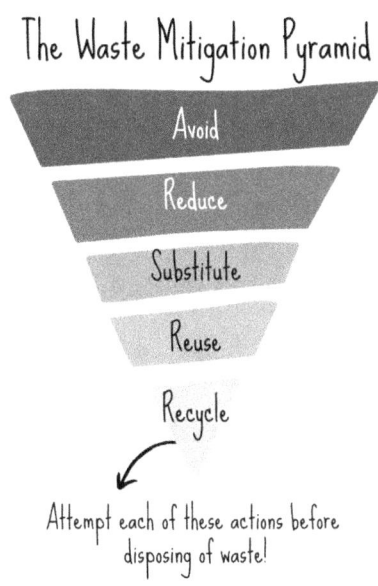

The Waste Mitigation Pyramid
- Avoid
- Reduce
- Substitute
- Reuse
- Recycle

Attempt each of these actions before disposing of waste!

While proper waste collection is a critical step to better managing waste, waste avoidance is the bigger goal. The less we bring into our households, the less we must dispose. A pervasive throwaway culture has caused us to generate excess waste when we tire of the things we buy, or they prematurely break or wear out because they are not made to last. As a global society, we buy things impulsively. We buy more than we need. We are addicted to consumerism, and our shopping habits are never satisfied. Overconsumption doesn't just harm us individually but affects our planet. We need to be smart about what we buy.

We rarely think about the resources and materials required to produce almost everything. That means not only are we trashing that leftover lasagna from Tuesday night, but we are also tossing out the water and cow feed used to produce the beef and cheese, as well as the fuel used to transport the noodles to the grocery store. The US Department of Agriculture (USDA) estimates Americans waste a third of the food supply annually, which can be worth billions of dollars.

Almost everything will become a waste one day–we need to return to giving value to the things we own and use. This mindset will help us pay attention to our consumption habits and think about how they affect the environment.

Why live more sustainably?

Environmental degradation is not completely irreversible. Governments, industries, societies, and individuals must work together to shift course. Solving the world's environmental troubles will require significant changes in policies and regulations, business practices, and infrastructure. Individually, we must be conscious of our behavior and decisions that affect the environment.

We can't keep accepting the status quo–we need to minimize the resources we use and reduce our behavior's environmental impact. The need to take climate action is no longer only a conversation; it's reality! Let's give up consumption addiction. Before we buy, let's find out where and how it's produced. Let's ask what the manufacturer is doing to reduce its environmental impact. Before we trash something, let's consider the best way to offload it if it no longer serves us. Reuse it for another purpose? Repair it if it's broken? Donate or sell it to someone else who needs it? If the item is trash, let's consider where to dispose of it before putting it on the curb. Can you compost it? Recycle it? Be curious! Ask questions about production methods and where they go when discarded.

Ultimately, our failure to live more sustainably could cause a diminished quality of life for future generations. But Earth still has a chance. Consider this: in 20 or 30 years, do you want to look back and say you did what you could? Or that you regret your choices? We are all playing a part in our planet's future. Let's make our roles positive! We've injured Earth, but it has proven it can heal itself. So why aren't we doing more to help?

Reflect

If you had to explain to a child why protecting the planet matters, what would you say? How do your personal health and well-being connect to the health of the planet? If the Earth could speak, what do you think it would ask of you right now?

Chapter Takeaways

We are at a pivotal point in improving the health of our planet.

Sustainable living depends on focusing on three key areas: water use, energy use, and waste generation.

Conserving water and protecting water quality is paramount. Water is necessary for almost everything.

We need to use energy efficiently to minimize greenhouse gases and limit their impact on climate change.

Be conscious of what we buy. Waste avoidance is the goal, though proper waste collection and disposal is also a critical step to better managing waste.

CHAPTER 2

Why Aren't We Doing More to Save Earth?

> It is the greatest of all mistakes to do nothing because you can only do little.
>
> – SYDNEY SMITH

Overall, society is more educated about climate and the environment than ever before, but we are still running the marathon of shifting human behavior towards sustainability and protecting the environment. We know that making smarter, greener choices will have a positive impact, so why isn't everyone doing more to help the environment? If we can understand why we do the things we do (or don't do), we can learn how to change our behaviors and break through the "green glass ceiling."

Studies have tried to understand why environmentally conscious people don't act sustainably. Researchers have investigated why people end up hurting the environment they're trying to help. Here are a few of the common reasons people aren't making greener choices.

We don't think it's our responsibility.

A lack of environmental education can affect the way we view environmental issues. Beliefs about climate change run the spectrum from the skeptical and dismissive to the concerned and alarmist. This range of beliefs results in various opinions on how to address climate change. One study proposes that a belief in climate change does not correlate to pro-environmental behavior but is predictive of support for federal climate policies. Someone's belief in climate action doesn't translate into a belief that it's their responsibility to change things. The study offers that people are more apt to expect their government to take on the challenge. Depending on the country, some people may think it is less of their responsibility to improve because other countries pollute more.

Our lack of understanding of how we fit into larger-scale systems is another barrier to acting. Some people think that understanding their role in an ecosystem is unnecessary, but not knowing our connection to a wider process can be detrimental to our ability to contribute to environmental challenges. For example, excessive water use in home gardening can strain local water supply resources and carry fertilizers, pesticides, and other pollutants into local waterways. Disposal of pharmaceuticals through our sanitary systems also leads to water pollution and disrupts the balance of nutrients, harming aquatic ecosystems.

We don't see the urgency.

People don't always see environmental degradation with their own eyes if they aren't directly impacted by it. Droughts, unclean or lack of water, and extreme weather happen somewhere else. Since their personal environments aren't impacted, they don't feel a need or have a desire to change their behavior.

Governmental policy failures have also left citizens confused about what to do or the value of doing anything. For instance, existing policies financially reward environmentally damaging activities: wood in a forest has a greater value after it's cut, so deforestation continues. Conservation policies have become so partisan that thinking or acting in a certain way toward the environment lies with one political party versus another. This divisiveness results in policy challenges and blockages rather than collaboration toward improvement. Often, governments do not sufficiently consult communities about the seriousness of sustainability issues during policy development, so the public doesn't understand the urgent need for change. If our legislative policies and practices do not support improvement, they may convey that environmental conservation is not a priority.

We think our actions won't have a meaningful impact.

It's hard to imagine our actions making an impact amidst the actions of the other billions of people on the planet. Sure, remembering to take your reusable grocery bags to the market once, twice, or even a dozen times may not have a significant impact. But compounded over a lifetime, that same habit can make a massive difference. A factor we can forget about is the impact of time.

We use phantom energy to power our TV, game console, and other devices when they are plugged in but turned off, for example. Similarly, using cold water to wash clothes for a year will clean clothes just as well as hot water, help them last longer, and save the same amount of energy needed to charge a mobile phone for a *lifetime*. Little bits add up!

Acting sustainably isn't trendy in some communities either. People become discouraged from making a change if they think it won't be socially acceptable. They don't want to appear to be one of only a few acting. Research has shown that harnessing social influence is a remarkably effective way to change behavior. In 2010, the city of Calgary rolled out a program called grass-cycling where residents left their grass clippings to decompose naturally in the yard rather than bagging them for landfill disposal. Even though the city explained the environmental benefits of this sustainable behavior, initial adoption rates were low. The city changed its approach and put flyers on residents' doors expressing things like, "Your neighbors are grass-cycling. You can too." This social influencing tactic resulted in doubling the number of participants over two weeks.

Another way to think about it is that environmental damage didn't happen overnight. It resulted from consistent, small actions. Therefore, in the same way, restoring our environment's health will also take consistent actions. Don't underestimate the actions others are taking! On Earth Day a few years ago, my daughter and I picked up trash along the levee near our home. We filled a kitchen bag with wrappers, string, bags, paper, and other litter. Now, imagine 30 people had joined us. We would have been able to cover a greater area and fill many bags. The same holds true when you're switching off the lights and unplugging devices when you leave home. Millions of people are likely doing the same thing. Think of how impactful that is.

We think it costs more time and money.

Today's world stretches us for cash and time, so we prioritize how we spend both. There's a popular belief that "the costs of socially responsible consumption are greater than its benefits." More than half of a study's respondents thought a sustainable lifestyle is expensive. Average prices at specialized stores or for eco-friendly products are indeed higher than those of traditional stores or products. However, when considered from a life cycle perspective (meaning including raw materials, processing, manufacturing, distribution, use, and disposal), many environmentally friendly products are more cost-effective and efficient than their counterparts in the long run. Let's consider napkins.

Let's say you want to replace paper napkins with fabric ones. If you buy paper napkins in bulk, the cheapest pack might cost you around $3.00 for 500 napkins. A set of cotton napkins I could run $20 for 12. Making some assumptions, a family of four would use enough paper napkins to require six packs of 500 napkins per year.

Disposable napkins would cost about $20 annually, with around 2,600 paper napkins going to the landfill. The initial outlay for the set of cloth napkins would be the same as the annual cost of paper napkins. You'd recoup the initial investment in a year, save money, and eliminate landfill waste. Washing the reusable napkins with bathroom and kitchen towels would not require additional energy or water.

Reflect

What excuses or habits keep you from making more sustainable choices, and where do they come from? What role does convenience play in your daily decisions, and how does it conflict with sustainability? When have you felt inspired to act for the planet, and what helped you follow through (or not)?

Chapter Takeaways

We know we need to make smarter, greener choices to positively affect the environment, but we may still not make those choices for various reasons. We need to overcome these challenges.

Living sustainably doesn't need to be on trend for us to change our behavior. Dare to be different.

Sustainable living does not need to cost more or take more time.

PART TWO

Create Habits That Stick

This part of the book is the main feature–you'll find everything you need to get going and to create ecohabits that stick. This part covers:

The Anatomy of a Habit will help you understand how to harness the power of your brain to create new Earth-friendly behaviors.

Get Ready will help you find the reason you want to make a difference and will help you set your guiding principles.

Put Your Ecohabit Together will walk you through defining the trigger, routine, and reward parts of your new ecohabit and finding resources you'll need to harness the power of your ecohabit.

Ideas to Get You Started includes ecohabit ideas, broken down into their triggers, routines, and rewards and provides bonus advice plus sustainable swaps.

Anticipate and Overcome Obstacles will guide you in developing a Plan B for when things don't quite go as planned.

Define Success will help you set metrics to monitor progress.

Get Going! will teach you how to track your progress and adjust when needed.

Break Bad Habits will give you advice on how to turn a less eco-friendly habit into a new ecohabit.

I've created a set of worksheets to help you through the process of building your new ecohabits. They are available in the Appendix at the back of this book and as a free download:

- Planning My New Ecohabit
- Preparing for Obstacles
- Progress Checks (Daily and Weekly)
- Breaking Unfriendly Habits
- Rebuilding Unfriendly Habits

Habits are habits, whatever you're trying to achieve! You can apply the lessons learned in this part to *anything*, not just living more sustainably.

CHAPTER 3

The Anatomy of a Habit

> Great things are not done by impulse, but by a series of small things brought together.
>
> – VINCENT VAN GOGH

You know something needs to change to improve the quality of our environment, so why does it seem so hard to make eco-friendly choices stick? Blame it on your brain.

Your brain spends energy to run your body whether you are doing something natural like breathing or something specific like talking to someone. Because every action takes energy, your brain wants to spend as little time as possible thinking about how to operate your body so it can conserve energy. Your brain helps you deal with all of life's demands by creating habits. Habits protect you from decision fatigue.

You have everyday routines like waking up and brushing your teeth, eating the same meal at your favorite restaurant, and driving the same route to work each morning. Your brain doesn't spend much energy thinking about how to do these activities because they are habits. One night at the dinner table recently, both my kids said that when they grew up, they'd remember how every night I brewed myself a hot cup of coffee and curled up to read a book before bed. I didn't even realize I had built that habit in a way that was so noticeable to others. It was rote; something I didn't even think about doing. How did my nightly relaxation activity become a habit?

Experts have researched habits for years from various perspectives. In reviewing their research, I've found that three key parts make up a habit: a trigger, a routine, and a reward. Understanding each of these parts and how they work will help you build new habits or change old ones.

THE ANATOMY OF A HABIT

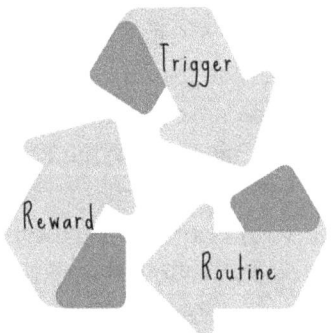

The trigger

A variety of familiar context clues trigger habits. Location, activities taking place, people around us, time of day, and our emotional state can all be cues to trigger a habit. Let's go back to my "coffee and a book" habit my kids brought up. Every night after we clean up the kitchen from the calamity of making dinner, I take a moment to relax and unwind in my corner of the couch. This pause lets me clear my mind of the day's craziness and get off my tired feet for a moment. My brain slows down and stops running through the laundry list of things to do. This post-dinner transition period is my "coffee and a book" trigger. This is the only time of day my brain triggers this habit. I've tried sitting on the couch with my coffee and a book after breakfast on Sunday mornings, but I end up watching whatever show the kids have on TV or endlessly scrolling through social media on my phone. The habit doesn't trip.

Triggers work best if they are simple and happen in the location where the routine will take place. Something as simple as a Post-It Note or alarm (also known as a context prompt) can help get things going. Let's look at my kitchen recycling bag as a context prompt. My husband keeps our recycling bin in the alley on the side of our house. It's inconvenient to go out to the bin every time we have something to recycle. Because of this, the item will probably end up in the kitchen trash can. To make things easier, I bought a small hanging recycling bag and placed it in one of our kitchen's bottom cabinets, since we generate most of our recyclables there. Now we have a receptacle at our fingertips to remind us to recycle. When the bag gets full, my son empties it into the outside bin. Another behavior you already do (also known as an action prompt) can remind you to act out the new routine afterward. Here's an example of an action prompt as a trigger.

One way of conserving water is to turn off the faucet while you brush your teeth. It's hard to remember to do because leaving the water running has become a habit for many people! I recently started using an electric toothbrush and decided to build a new habit of turning off the water. Switching ON the toothbrush is my trigger to turn OFF the water. It took a few tries to get going, but now I'm consistent with it. Something else that helps with my habit is when I hear both the water and the brush running. It's louder when they're both turned on, and the sounds remind me to shut off the water if I have forgotten.

Think of a habit you have. Can you name the trigger?

The routine

The routine is the behavior kicked off by the trigger. Back to "coffee and a book": once my brain triggers me to quiet down, it can switch to devouring whatever story I've been reading. I sit in my corner of the couch with a warm mug in hand to check out of reality for a bit. Routines can be simple, like mine, or complex. In the recycling example, the routine is placing the can or junk mail into the bag.

The goal for a routine should be to engage in behavior versus trying to stop behavior. The problem with defining goals to stop something is that when you succeed, you have done nothing. If your brain triggers a habit, it pushes hard to enact the routine. Triggering your brain to stop doesn't kick off a routine. In comparison, it takes more effort and energy to stop doing something than to do it.

When triggering a stop habit, the brain must first find the reason you shouldn't be taking an action. Then it must engage the need to focus and exert mental effort to stop. Remember, the brain is trying to use the least amount of energy it can! Think of it this way; it's easier to start a rock rolling down a hill than it is to stop one.

The reward

Your brain doesn't store all the behaviors you've done more than once as habits. It remembers only the ones with a positive connotation. Incentives and rewards help the brain store behaviors as habits. They can be physical or emotional sensations. Your belly feels full after eating a healthy breakfast. Your spirits soar as you cross the finish line of the race you've been training for. People are more likely to repeat behaviors when they receive positive feedback, whether that feedback is internally (like congratulating themselves) or externally provided (like someone else congratulating them). Research has shown that hope and pride in something help drive environmentally friendly behavior. Your brain doesn't just use these rewards to remember habits; it craves them. The more you perform a behavior that rewards your brain, the more your brain will want to repeat that behavior.

It's central for the reward associated with a new habit to be something that won't lose its potency. Treating yourself with a piece of cake every time you turn off the water while brushing your teeth won't help you build your water-saving habit in the long run (though it may help you build your dental bill!). Developing good habits will be most successful when you do them for their own sake, and you gain satisfaction from what you've achieved, tapping into the reward circuitry of your brain.

B.J. Fogg gives a sweet example in his book *Tiny Habits*. Have you ever seen a baby trying to walk for the first time? The baby will pull herself up and take those first tentative steps. And what do the onlookers do? Cheer like mad! I recall the video of my daughter taking her first steps in our hallway–my husband, son, and I looked like lunatics clapping our hands and hollering our excitement as she moved from one end to the other. At one point, she stopped and clapped for herself too!

Celebrating causes your brain to recognize and encode the behavior you recently performed. Celebrating the successful completion of the trigger-routine-reward loop will cement positive recognition into your brain. Find a celebration to do in the moment that works for you–even if it feels silly. You are doing something worth celebrating! You should recognize that you are positively changing your life and the world. These fun mini celebrations will also help to keep your motivation up.

My intrinsic desire to recycle metal, plastic, and paper is the "feel good" reward that encouraged me to start our home recycling effort. I receive no immediate reward when I put an aluminum can into the bag. However, I know I am helping the environment by having my cans and bottles take a road trip to the recycling center versus ending their lives in the landfill. Now that my recycling behavior is a habit, the emotional reward is less important in driving my behavior. It's second nature. Seeing the amount of recyclables we put on the curb each week for pickup has led me to consider how we can reduce the volume of recyclable materials we bring into our home. Habits breed more habits.

Recall the trigger you found. Think about whether external or internal rewards drive the routine it kicks off. Will the reward stand the test of time? Or are you just eating cake? Without understanding how habits work, you can't successfully adjust your behavior. Knowing how triggers and rewards affect our routines will help set the stage for successful change.

Reflect

Which ecohabits feel automatic to you now, and how did they become second nature? Have you ever changed a habit because of someone else's influence? What helped you stay consistent?

Chapter Takeaways

To conserve energy, your brain wants to spend as little time as possible thinking about how to operate your body. Your brain does this by creating habits.

Habits comprise three key parts: the trigger, the routine, and the reward.

Familiar context clues such as location, other activities taking place, people around you, time of day, and emotional state trigger habits.

Triggers kick off routines and should engage behavior versus stop behavior.

The brain remembers routines with positive connotations, so rewards associated with new habits need to carry weight and endure over time.

CHAPTER 4

Get Ready

Habit is second nature.

– CICERO

You already have habits: good, bad, and indifferent. Each of them started with a conscious decision. The more often you made that choice, the easier it became until you reached the point where you didn't consciously decide anymore–it was automatic. It had become a habit. We've all attempted–and even been successful at–breaking "bad" habits (cursing, nail biting) and creating new ones (eating healthy, exercising). Remember? It took effort and time. Creating eco-habits will be the same. A lifetime of trashing recyclables or letting the water run while you brush your teeth won't change overnight, but this chapter can help you get going.

In the last chapter, you learned how the brain craves habits to save energy, and you understand the parts that make up a habit. Now, let's put that knowledge to work.

This chapter covers the following key things you'll need to do to prepare for successfully making a change:
- Finding your Why
- Identifying your starting point
- Defining your North Star

Find your Why

Finding the motivation behind your new habit before you try to change things is critical. The brain will want to circumvent your new plans. Your built-in motivational system will want to continue to promote old behaviors because, technically, they are still successful even though they are directing you away from your new goals. Your brain doesn't know whether a habit is good or bad–it only knows whether it's completing a routine.

Before I talk about setting goals, think about why making this change is important to you. Will it get you somewhere you want to be? Are you doing it to satisfy your desires? Changing habits will take time and effort. You want your time and effort to go into something meaningful to you. Something worth it. Imagine yourself at 75 or 80, or when your grandchildren are grown up. How do you think life on Earth will look then? What part of that picture bothers you the most? What would be most meaningful to you if it were different?

Here are a few reasons to live more sustainably that might give you ideas to help you define your Why:
- Reducing pollution
- Conserving natural resources
- Preserving biodiversity

- Reducing human exposure to pollutants
- Improving public health
- Enabling future generations' access to clean air, water, and fertile land
- Saving money

Throughout the rest of the book, I'll use the example of recycling aluminum cans to illustrate each step of the process. When I think about my Why, the following things related to the life cycle impact of aluminum production come to mind:

- Mining aluminum ore requires removing native vegetation, leading to a loss of habitat and food for local wildlife, as well as causing soil erosion.
- The leftover sludge from mining ore can seep into aquifers and contaminate water supplies.
- Processing the ore into metal aluminum creates greenhouse gases and releases toxic air pollutants, creating smog.
- Metals like aluminum and steel can be recycled infinitely without losing quality or purity.

It's critical to build your Why on something positive. Guilt can be an effective motivator, but it is a complicated emotional tool. Psychologists proved that using guilt as a motivator results in less desirable behavior in the long term. You want building new ecohabits to be a positive experience! It won't help if you're continually guilting yourself into performing the habit or reminding yourself how awful you are if you don't choose your new routine. All that negative self-talk will wear you down; you'll get fed up and give up on your new habit.

Having a powerful motivation to do something different will help you stay the course when times are tough until your routine becomes a habit. If your reason for changing is flimsy, your brain will bully you into executing the old habit. It will suggest that the effort for this new behavior isn't worth it or that you won't achieve what you want if you aren't seeing tangible results immediately. Pull out your *Planning My New Ecohabit* worksheet and write down your Why, so you can reflect on it when you get stuck.

> **My Why:**
>
> I want to protect Earth's natural beauty and biodiversity. Seeing holes torn in the Earth from mining makes me sad.

Establish the starting point

Before starting any change journey, you need to know your starting point. Defining an endpoint isn't helpful if you don't know how far away it is from where you are now or in what direction you need to travel. A straightforward way to understand where you are now is to figure out your environmental footprint baseline. Different calculators can tell you with a few inputs what your carbon, energy, water use, or waste generation footprint is. Below are a few examples. The output of these calculators is a credible place to find room for improvement. (Hint, hint: a new ecohabit idea!)

Alternatively, you might already know what you want to work on. Your water bill shows that your water use is out of control, or your family complains about food waste. That works! Start there. Do what fits your life.

Ecological Footprint: The Global Footprint Network calculates your ecological footprint, which compares your resource demand against Earth's ability for biological regeneration. It tells you the number of Earths you would need to counteract the impact of your lifestyle. https://www.footprintcalculator.org/

Energy Use: The US's Energy Star Home Energy Yardstick can compare your home's energy efficiency with that of comparable homes. First, you'll need a year of utility bills. Answering a few questions will give you your home's score, insights into how much of your energy use relates to heating and cooling versus other uses, an estimate of your home's carbon footprint, and a set of recommendations. https://www.energystar.gov/campaign/home-energy-yardstick

Carbon Footprint: Completing ClimateHero's Carbon Calculator takes about five minutes and is divided into three sections to estimate your carbon footprint: housing, travel, and consumption. It not only provides you estimated carbon footprint but tells you in what aspects of your life you're doing well and where you can improve. Multiple countries are available. https://carbon-calculator.climatehero.org/

Water Use: The US-based Water Footprint Calculator estimates both your direct water use at home plus indirect use from travel, shopping and recycling habits, diet, pets, and more. https://watercalculator.org/

Waste Generation: Montgomery County, Maryland provides simple tips to conduct a waste audit. By doing a home waste audit, you can understand what you consume and the waste you generate. The process is messy (get your gloves!), but this understanding helps you identify patterns and areas for improvement. https://mygreenmontgomery.org/project/conduct-a-home-waste-audit/

Define your North Star

Now that you have a feel for your starting point and a bit of motivation, the next step is to figure out what you want to achieve from your new habit. Your footprint results will give you several ideas for improvement, but you may have other ideas too. You might have behaviors that bug you or that you know are unhelpful. Those are respectable places to start. Keep those in mind and think broadly. What do you want to accomplish on a large scale? Envision something that would stand out if you could do it well. Just because you can't reach the goal today doesn't mean it's unreachable. GO BIG! Think about how you can live today, knowing what matters in the big picture. Setting a North Star means intentionally choosing the direction that leads you to your long-term success.

Workable ideas include reducing electricity or water use at your home. Alone, these ideas aren't ecohabits because you haven't yet established the specific actions needed to build into a routine. When you have a standout North Star ready, write it in your *Planning My New Ecohabit* worksheet. Make sure it's something you are interested in and want to work on versus something you should do. Now that you have your North Star in hand, let's work on building your new habit.

> **My North Star:**
>
> I want to help reduce virgin material use by reusing and recycling materials already in circulation.

Reflect

What does "saving the Earth" mean to you personally? How does it connect to your values or lifestyle? What emotions come up when you think about the planet's future? How can those feelings motivate action?

Chapter Takeaways

Finding the motivation behind your new habit before you try to change things is critical because your brain will want to circumvent these new plans.

Knowing your Why will help you stay the course when times are tough until you establish your new ecohabit.

Know your starting point before starting any journey.

Knowing how you can live today and how it fits into the big picture will help to set up a standout North Star.

CHAPTER 5

Put Your Ecohabit Together

> Character is simply habit long continued.
>
> – PLUTARCH (modernized)

Now it's time to plan out your new ecohabit. Your North Star was probably broad and abstract, so now it's time to break it down into meaningful actions you can take routinely. When you complete an activity related to a goal, it signals to the brain that it's time to learn and start building habits. This chapter will guide you through identifying the trigger, routine, and reward parts of your ecohabit so you can construct a clear, action-oriented behavior change.

Define the routine & find the resources you need

While your goals can be broad, the routine part of your habit needs to be specific enough to tell when you have completed it. *Recycle more* is a nice goal, but it's not a promising routine. *Recycle metal cans instead of throwing them into the trash bin* is a better, more active possibility for a routine. The short-term action is straightforward, and it will move you towards the longer-term goal of recycling more. You now may have several options you can tackle to move towards your North Star. Nice! Pick one to start. Evidence shows that trying to make several changes at once is not as effective as focusing on one new thing at a time. Once you build your first new ecohabit, you can always go back for more.

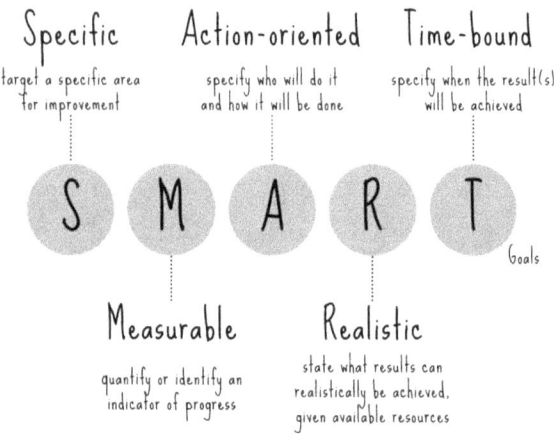

It's crucial to set routines small enough and specific enough to allow you to sustain behavior in the long run. Your brain favors immediate rewards over long-term gains, like improving the environment's health, in comparison to quick actions, such as recycling. To help counteract this bias, you'll need to frame your longer-term goal in a way that produces measurable wins in the short term but directs you toward longer-term success. This way, there's less competition in your brain.

Smaller actions work because they're easy to do, keep you motivated, and are measurable. Smaller steps will also lead you to further progress as you build upon them. It's naturally hard to start something new, but once you overcome the initial inertia, the momentum keeps you moving. You may need to explore different options when defining your routine, depending on what your North Star is. Whatever you decide, match the behaviors to you. They need to be things you *want* to do, and you *can* do. If composting is not something you're up for or don't have space for–don't! Find a community composting site or give your compostables to a friend who composts. If your town isn't biker-friendly, it's too far to bike to work, or you physically can't bike, find another way to reduce your commuting emissions.

You can create ecohabits by changing the tools you use in a routine or by changing your action. Swapping the tools in an unfriendly habit for friendlier ones is the simplest way to make a change. I have a stack of fabric napkins in a container on our kitchen table. The default choice at my house is reusable napkins. I don't buy paper napkins anymore! When we switched to fabric, the routine didn't change. The trigger (eating at the kitchen table), routine (taking a napkin), and reward (clean fingers) are the same as before. I only replaced the tool used to carry out the routine. I invested upfront in the napkins, but I've already received a return on my investment as discussed earlier. Since the napkins are reusable, I'm saving a few things:

- Money, since I'm no longer buying paper napkins routinely.

- Resources, since no additional trees are harvested, processed, and bleached, and no added water or energy is used to create the napkins that then need to be delivered to my store, using more energy.
- Waste, since I'm not sending added trash to the landfill from the packaging or used paper napkins (not to mention any waste generated by the paper napkin production process).
- Since my fabric napkins are getting washed with my towels, I'm not using more water, energy, or soap to clean them.

An example of a changing your action within the routine part of a habit is turning the lights off when leaving a room. There is no tool to swap out here (unless you've enlisted the help of a smart plug or other smart home device, that is). Establishing an effective trigger and reward will help drive the action of the routine. The beauty of setting action-based routines is that there's no clear endpoint. This kind of habit will become part of how you live your day-to-day life. You won't get to a point where you say, "Well, I've turned off enough lights. It's time to stop!" You'll have built a new habit to sustain your behavior for the long term. Focusing on an endpoint will not cause lasting change. Remember, your action-based routine needs to be engaging–it needs you to do something, not stop doing something.

> **My Routine:**
>
> Collect and recycle all the aluminum waste that comes into my home each week, like drink cans, food cans, and foil products

When you've identified your new routine, put it down in your *Planning My New Ecohabit* worksheet. Before you move on, here are a few things to think about to set yourself up to complete the routine when it's triggered:

> Do I have the resources to take this action successfully?
>
> Do I know the right way to take this action?
>
> How often will I need to do this?
>
> What changes can I make to disrupt old habits?

Think about the physical space, the supplies, the services, or the knowledge you may need to complete your routine. If you plan to recycle metal cans in your house, do you have a recycling bin? Do you have the space in your kitchen for one? How will you dispose of the cans when the bin is full? Does your town provide curbside recycling? Or will you need to drive to a collection center? Do the cans need to be rinsed clean? Or can they have food remnants? You won't be able to complete the routine without knowing these things and managing your environment to support the new habit.

Don't forget to think about the people around you as well. Will they support you or deter you from your desire to help the planet? Make a list of allies you can turn to when the going gets tough. Jot down any resources you'll need in the Resource section of your *Planning My New Ecohabit* worksheet.

> **My Resources:**
>
> Recycling bin
> List of accepted materials
> Recycling contract
> Curbside pickup day

Identify the trigger and manage your environment

Once you have the routine set, it's time to think about how you'll trigger it. How will you fit the new ecohabit into your life? Ask yourself these questions about your routine:

When will this take place?

Where will it take place?

What other activities are taking place during or before my trigger?

What will remind me to carry out these steps when I need to?

The surrounding environment heavily influences your behavior. Examine ways to set up your environment to help make triggering the routine easy. You may already have triggers in place for an old routine. Will these triggers work for your new habit as well?

One helpful exercise is to physically go to where you will commonly need to trigger your new routine. Refer to your Resources list and look around. Think about how you could set up the space to support the new ecohabit. Can you set up reminders to help you kick off the routine?

Remember the recycling bag example? To help my family remember to recycle food cans or paper junk mail, I put a recycling bag on one of our bottom kitchen cabinet doors. We cook meals and open our mail in the kitchen, near that bag. It's easy for my husband or me to drop in an envelope quickly when we don't have to go far to do it. Do you think we'd have built that habit if the recycling bag were outside or in the garage?

Managing your environment and triggers will give you a better chance of completing your routine. Your environment is a powerful driver of what you do because there is a consistent mapping between your behaviors and the surroundings. Use the Resources you've identified to set a plan for your trigger. When you've come up with a trigger you're satisfied with, write it in your *Planning My New Ecohabit* worksheet.

My Triggers:

An empty food can
The recycling bag in my kitchen
(context prompts)

Define your reward

Rewards can be a variety of things and should positively compensate you for your efforts. This positive reinforcement will teach your brain that this behavior is something you want to do again. As mentioned in *Chapter 3: The Anatomy of a Habit*, be careful with rewards. You don't want to get caught up with external motivations (like rewarding yourself with a gift every time you complete your new routine). Once those external incentives go away, your habit likely will too. External incentives undermine intrinsic desires to adopt a new behavior. This is especially relevant to building ecohabits–you want to change your behavior so it affects our planet positively. Sometimes the only reward for completing the routine is the satisfaction that it matters. To help this positive feedback reinforce the behavior into a habit, you can use a mini celebration, like doing a happy dance.

Here are a few mini celebration ideas borrowed from *Tiny Habits*:

- When you remember to use your reusable straw and reject the plastic one from the restaurant, you can nod your head.
- When you chuck an aluminum soda can into the recycle bin instead of the trashcan, say "Swish!" and pump your fist like you just made a basketball goal.
- When you receive your power bill and see your energy use has gone down, imagine seeing fireworks.

- If you gather litter while on your morning walk, hum a cheery tune to yourself.
- When you remember to take your reusable shopping bags to the grocery store, smile big.

Find a celebration to do in the moment that works for you–even if it feels silly. You are doing something worth celebrating! These fun mini celebrations will also help to keep your motivation up. Write your chosen reward on your *Planning My New Ecohabit* worksheet once you've identified it, even if it's just a good feeling.

As much as you prepare, things won't always go to plan. Think ahead about obstacles you may run into and how you might overcome them to keep your ecohabits growing. We'll talk about derailers in the next chapter.

> **My Rewards:**
>
> Satisfaction of emptying my kitchen bag full of cans into the outside bin and seeing a full recycle bin on the curb on recycling pickup day

Reflect

What cues could you redirect in your day to spark more sustainable routines? When you make an eco-friendly choice, what reward do you feel: emotional, social, or practical?

Chapter Takeaways

The routine: Your ecohabit's routine needs to be specific enough for you to know when you've completed it and small enough to allow you to sustain behavior in the long run.

The trigger: The surrounding environment heavily influences your behavior, so look at ways to set up your environment to make your ecohabit easy to do.

The reward: Positive reinforcement will teach your brain that this behavior or action is something it wants to do again.

CHAPTER 6

Ideas to Get You Started

> Look and listen for the welfare of the whole people and have always in view not only the present but also the coming generations.
>
> – GREAT LAW OF THE IROQUOIS (modernized)

If you're looking for ecohabit suggestions, you're in the right place. You know your lifestyle, the places you frequent, and your behavior. If an idea doesn't resonate with you, make up your own or customize one here to fit your life with what you have. These ideas align with the topics in *Chapter 1: Why save Earth?*: conserve and protect water, conserve energy, and reduce waste. Breaking them down into the anatomical parts of a habit allows you to assess how to implement the ecohabit into your lifestyle. After each section, I also provide a few Sustainable Swaps for you to consider in addition to your new ecohabit. You can find a list of other resources at the end of the chapter.

Conserve and protect water

Over time, humans have proven we are inefficient at using water. The average person in the US uses 80-100 gallons of water a day for indoor use. Toilets are the biggest water users at home. Baths and showers come in second place. Plus, the average US household wastes over 10,000 gallons of water per year from leaks from dripping faucets and running toilets. That's a lot of water! Imagine 10,000 milk jugs! Cutting down on water use and leaks will not only help the environment, but it will also help our wallets.

You learned in Chapter 1 that while water covers about three-quarters of Earth's surface, less than 1% of that water is usable. Water scarcity is a reality for many communities across the globe. As the world's population increases, water use grows. We must consider the impact on water from our purchases and other activities besides being aware of how much water we use. We want to minimize our contribution to negative water quality and limited water availability.

Idea: Take a quick shower instead of a bath and reuse your bath towels

A 10 minute shower with a low-flow showerhead uses almost half the water as an average bath does. An easy way to cut water use and ensure a shorter shower is to set a timer or turn on a playlist with only a couple of energetic songs on it. Then when you're done scrubbing, don't throw your used towel directly into the laundry hamper. Reuse your towel multiple times before you wash it. Using a towel several times before washing it will save water and energy plus detergents. Be sure to hang it up to dry well in between uses so it doesn't stink up. I swap out our bath towels weekly if they aren't smelly.

Trigger: You're stinky and dirty after a hard day working in the garden.

Routine: Set a 10 minute timer on your phone and hop in the shower.

Reward: A squeaky-clean feeling in the moment and a lower water bill at the end of the month.

Bonus Advice: If your shower water takes a while to heat, time yours after someone else's, taking advantage of the pre-heated water.

Idea: Turn off the water when you're brushing your teeth or washing your hands

Why do some of us leave the water running while we brush our teeth or wash our faces? We've all done it, but it's wasteful. Turning off the water while brushing your teeth can save up to 3,000 gallons of water a year-that's 40 bathtubs filled to the rim. Turn it back on when you need to rinse.

Trigger: It's time to brush your teeth, and you have toothpaste on your toothbrush.

Routine: Turn on the water to wet the brush, then immediately turn it off.

Reward: Minty, fresh breath in the moment, and a lower water bill in the long term.

Idea: Wash your dishes efficiently either by hand or with a dishwasher

Like brushing your teeth with the water running, it's inefficient to wash dishes one by one under running water. Use the classic method of dishwashing instead: fill one side of a double sink with water and soap for washing and the other side with water for rinsing. If you have a single sink, use a separate washtub for either washing or rinsing.

Run a full dishwasher load on a cycle that's right for what you're washing. Most dishwashers have different load settings depending on how dirty the dishes are (pots/pans, light wash, even energy saving cycles on some machines). Instead of using the heated dry setting, air dry the dishes with the dishwasher door open.

Trigger: You have a few dirty dishes after a meal.

Routine: Scrape and lightly rinse off any larger food bits and set the plates in the dishwasher until it gets full. (Alternatively, you could hand wash and air dry them using the classic method described above.)

Reward: Clean dishes and lower energy and water bills at the end of the month.

Idea: Adjust your gardening habits to save water

The EPA estimates Americans waste as much as 4.5 billion gallons of water each day for landscape irrigation. That's the same as 12 minutes of water rushing over Niagara Falls. A first step in reducing irrigation water is to plant drought tolerant native species that can handle dry conditions. When it comes time to water your garden, water early in the morning or after sunset when the day is cooler. Watering at these times prevents water from evaporating during the heat of the day. More will reach your plants, and they'll have a better chance of absorbing it. Don't over-water; plants will only absorb as much as they need, and you will waste the over-watering.

Using recycled water will cut down on freshwater consumption. My mother-in-law suggests collecting rainwater in a bucket or barrel for garden and potted plant watering. Collect shower water while you're waiting for it to warm up and use it in the yard later. Water collection is especially helpful if your area is going through a dry spell or drought. I've even heard of people saving water from cooking pasta or rinsing rice and beans to water plants. This water has nutrients and starches from the foods and can aid plants' growth.

Trigger: *You come home from work and notice the potted plants on your porch are looking thirsty.*

Routine: *After dinner, water the plants while you catch up with your partner or family outside.*

Reward: *A lush garden without wasted water.*

Bonus Advice: Don't use water to wash off sidewalks or porches; a simple broom works fine.
Bonus Advice: Mulch your garden to keep water from evaporating.

Sustainable Swaps to conserve water

- Replace your existing toilet with a low-flow model. Alternatively, put a 2 liter or gallon sized bottle filled with water in the tank (away from the moving parts) to reduce the tank volume, resulting in less water consumed per flush.
- Only flush when necessary if you're comfortable with it. If it's yellow, let it mellow. Only flush Number 2.
- Swap your shower heads or faucet aerators with low-flow models.
- Replace your spray garden irrigation system with a drip system. Spray systems put out more water than

the ground can absorb, while drip systems release water at a slower rate. Be sure to set any irrigation system on a timer.
- Swap your hose and nozzle for a watering can when gardening. The watering can has a limited volume, and you don't risk over-watering.
- Leave lawn clipping on the grass instead of bagging; this cools the ground and keeps moisture.
- Select unbleached paper products like napkins and coffee filters, if you're still using paper, instead of the bleached versions. Bleaching consumes more energy and water and uses toxic compounds like chlorine, which can leach into the water system if not properly managed.

Conserve energy

Chapter 1 taught you that the world's increasing demand for fossil fuels to create energy contributes to climate change. As living standards, economies, and populations grow, so does the level of greenhouse gases in the atmosphere. These gases contribute to the global temperature rise, which is already wreaking havoc on our environment. We must scrutinize our energy use (and waste) to lower personal energy needs, decreasing greenhouse gas emissions.

Idea: Adjust your transportation methods and travel plans to reduce fuel use

According to the US Energy Information Administration, in 2023 Americans used roughly 137 billion gallons of motor gasoline to drive their cars and light trucks, enough for a vehicle to circle the equator 130 million times. Walking and biking are noble alternatives to fuel-driven vehicles. However, weather, location, and traffic conditions aren't always conducive to walking or biking to your destination.

Public transportation such as busses, streetcars, trolleys, and trains is already active. A bus driver will follow the route whether anyone is at the stop waiting for the bus to arrive. Capitalize on these "free" emissions! Another choice is to hitch a ride with friends and coworkers. My friend Michael lives within a mile of four girls who attend his daughter's school fourteen miles away. Sharing carpool duties is not only an easy way to save time for each family, but it also saves fuel from two daily trips per kid.

Sometimes, you just need to drive yourself somewhere. Plan the most efficient trip you can. Cut out unnecessary single-stop outings by combining trips. Strategically map out your errands to make the most efficient use of your time and fuel when you're heading to a certain part of town. It's easy to do, even if it's only in your head (I like to jot down stops in order on a scrap of paper, so I don't forget). Use your phone's GPS to find the shortest, most efficient routes during non-peak hours if possible–you'll reach your destination faster, and stop and go traffic won't trap you and kill your fuel efficiency.

Trigger: *You need a loaf of bread to make sandwiches for tomorrow's lunches, and your prescription is ready at the pharmacy.*

Routine: *Think about other errands you may need to run or places you plan to go before you jump in the car to head to the grocery and the pharmacy. Decide to buy the bread and medicine on your way back from the gym later this evening, since they are all near one another.*

Reward: *One trip to get everything you need.*

Bonus Advice: Empty your trunk of all the junk you've been hauling around. Increased weight in your vehicle requires more fuel.

Bonus Advice: Check your tire pressure. Reduced tire pressure requires more fuel to get your car moving. Refer to your vehicle's manual for recommended tire inflation levels.

Idea: Set the thermostat a few degrees higher in summer or lower in winter

One of the easiest ways to save energy, money, and the environment during the colder months is to lower the thermostat in your home by 2°F. A basic rule of thumb is to set the thermostat to 68°F (20°C) while you're at home in winter (and layer clothes if you get cold). Drop it 10 to 15°F lower before leaving the house for at least eight hours (like when you go to work or on vacation) and when you're asleep (you can bundle up in bed). Reverse your ceiling fan's direction to push warm air down. Doing all this can save up to 15% a year on the amount of energy used to heat your home, according to the US Department of Energy.

Similarly, in warmer months, set the temperature around 78°F (26°C) when you're at home (and use a fan to circulate the air) and push it to 85°F (29°C) while you're gone. Not only will doing this save energy, but it will save money in warmer months by making these adjustments. Of course, the setting you choose will depend on the age of your home and the efficiency of its insulation and windows.

> *Trigger:* Picking up your keys to leave the house for the day.
>
> *Routine:* Adjust the setting on the thermostat.
>
> *Reward:* Knowledge in the moment that you're saving energy, reinforced when the lower bill comes at the end of the month.

Bonus Advice: Keep your windows, shades, curtains, or blinds closed to insulate your home from daytime heat in warmer months. Keep them open to allow sunlight to warm your home in colder months. You won't have to set your thermostat as high or low.

Idea: Use alternative heating/cooling sources instead of your primary system

Sometimes there's no need to heat or cool the entire house if you're only using a small portion of it for a significant time. For example, my coworker Katie works from home in a small room in her house. Since everyone else in her family is at work or school during the day, there's no need for her to heat the upstairs or other living areas. She sets her thermostat for away as described in the previous idea. To combat getting cold during cooler months, she keeps a small electric space heater and a sweater handy. She will open the window if the weather is pleasant and turn on the ceiling fan to keep the air moving and to cool down. The electric fan and heater use much less energy than the full heating/cooling system does to heat the entire downstairs.

> *Trigger*: *You get cold/hot after adjusting the thermostat settings in the earlier idea.*
>
> *Routine*: *Turn on a space heater or fan instead of adjusting the central system.*
>
> *Reward*: *You're more comfortable in the room you're in.*

Idea: Use alternative or more efficient lighting options

I'm sure you've seen the classic photos of Earth at night showing light from all parts of the world. Society spends at least $50 billion globally on energy costs to produce light that escapes into space. Here are several ways to reduce light energy waste.

Use sunlight to brighten a room instead of overhead lighting by opening window coverings. Foregoing the overhead light results in less electricity use and is beneficial for your health too. Natural light improves comfort levels and mood. Open window blinds supply enough light for me to work every day. If I require a bit of extra illumination, I turn on a desk lamp with one low-wattage bulb to light my workspace instead of turning on the overhead light with four bulbs that illuminates the entire room. Similarly, I rarely turn on the overhead light in my living room because sunlight and a table lamp supply enough lighting at any time of day.

Several of my neighbors turn on the outdoor lighting even when they are home. It's helpful to have lights on at night when you arrive home late, but it's unnecessary for those lights to be turned on for all the darker hours, sending wasted light energy into the universe. If you're in for the evening and aren't expecting guests, turning off the outdoor lighting may take away a lovely ambiance, but it's saving energy. Alternatively, install night sky friendly lighting.

> *Trigger:* You walk into your living room Saturday morning to have a cup of coffee and read for a while.
>
> *Routine:* Open the window blinds or curtains instead of reaching for the light switch.
>
> *Reward:* Pleasant ambient light to start your day in a cheerful mood.

Idea: Wash and dry your laundry efficiently

Washing and drying clothes, towels, and bedding can use a lot of energy and water. Washing full loads saves energy and water by reducing the number of cycles you run. Even if you have the water level set to only fill the tub halfway for smaller loads, the cycle will use the same amount of energy. Cold water could save 90% of the energy per load versus using hot water. Cold water will wash your clothes just as well and could save you cash on your energy bill.

Similarly, dry full loads and check your load partway through the cycle to see if the items are dry enough to come out. Sometimes I find my dryer has time left on the timer, but the clothes are dry. Don't forget to clean the lint trap after every load! Not only is an overfilled trap a fire hazard, but it also reduces the dryer's air flow and drying efficiency, causing the cycle to use more energy.

If you have the space, hang clothes to dry or use a drying rack instead of using the dryer. You can do this indoors or outside if the weather allows. Even if you only hang dry laundry outside during warmer months or only line-dry bulky items like towels and blankets, you're still saving energy in the long run.

Did You Know? Your dryer also heats your home through radiative heat, causing your air conditioning to work harder.

Trigger: You washed a full load of towels that is ready to be dried.

Routine: You hang the towels outside on a clothesline to dry instead of popping them into the dryer.

Reward: Fresh smelling, sun-dried towels.

Sustainable Swaps to conserve energy

- If you have a choice of power providers, swap to a renewable energy provider (or one with more renewables in the mix).
- Drive or take the train instead of flying off on vacation.
- Swap your standard thermostat with a programmable one and set the program to lower or raise your setting automatically throughout the day.
- Swap traditional light bulbs for LEDs with lower wattage.
- Air dry your dishes instead of using the heated dry setting on your automatic dishwasher.
- Use a slow cooker or air fryer to cook a meal instead of heating the oven.
- Lower your water heater temperature setting to 120°F (38°C). For every degree lowered, you can conserve 3-5% of the energy required to heat your water.
- Increase your freezer temperature setting from 0°F (-18°C) to 5°F (-15°C) and you could save 5-7% of

annual energy usage and cost, and your food will be fine.
- Swap your gasoline powered yard equipment for electric or hand powered tools.

Reduce waste

Remember this factoid from Chapter 1:

> Humans generate over 2 billion tons of trash annually. That's the same weight as 12 million blue whales–the heaviest animal in the world!

The world is not large enough for all this waste to have a place for disposal. The first step in improving global waste management is to avoid generating it. We need to be smart about what we buy and what we can reuse or repurpose before it becomes waste.

Idea: Refuse single use products when out

Making smart decisions extends to when you are out, particularly when shopping or treating yourself to a meal. Single use plastics and similar materials are ubiquitous. You'll see them as shopping bags, cutlery, cups, receipts, wrappers, and more. It takes practice, but learn to say "No, thank you" to these items when offered, or take your sustainable alternative with you.

I've lost count of how many times I've said, "Plastic shopping bags are the bane of my existence!" People use plastic bags only once, and they usually throw them away instead of recycling them. Usually, they never make it to the landfill when thrown away and end up in our environment. If you're only buying a few things small enough to carry out of the store, there's no need for a bag. Another possibility is to request paper bags if available. Producing them requires less energy, and they can be reused, recycled, or composted if they aren't printed on or if they have been printed using plant-based inks. You can often fit more things in paper bags too, resulting in using fewer bags on your trip. Plus, they come from a renewable resource: trees!. Of course, you can take your reusable bag too! Stash them in useful places so remember to carry them into the store.

Say "No, thank you" to things like plastic straws, water bottles, or cutlery. The Ocean Conservancy reports more than a garbage truck's worth of plastics enters the ocean every minute. Use your own water bottle, travel mug, or reusable straw instead (or go without one!). Some places may even give you a discount for bringing in your own mug or cup. I have received funny looks when I reject a straw or remind my kids not to open them when automatically provided. But, I have received just as many kudos from wait staff for using my own brightly colored silicone straws.

> *Trigger*: *You decide to buy a cookie from a bakery while out in town. The server prepares to slip the cookie into a waxy sleeve before handing it to you.*
>
> *Routine*: *Say, "Oh, I don't need the wrapper; I'll throw it away. I'll take the cookie right from you."*
>
> *Reward*: *A yummy snack and no pristine wax sleeve to throw right into the trash can.*

Bonus Advice: In my area, Target, Lowe's, Walmart, and some grocery stores accept plastic bags for recycling, so check whether you can return them if you end up with any.

Idea: Choose products with sustainable packaging or products without packaging

Choose products with paper packaging where possible since paper is easily recyclable and less energy intensive to make. For example, buy eggs in a cardboard carton instead of a foam one. Cardboard is recyclable or compostable sometimes, while foam isn't. Skip the plastic baggies in the produce section and take along a reusable cotton net bag if you want to corral your items.

Trigger: You're shopping for lemons at the market.

Routine: Grab a few loose lemons instead of the ones in a plastic net bag.

Reward: No packaging to dispose of when you are home, and you can use the rinds to deodorize your sink's disposal or to exfoliate your skin.

Idea: Adjust how you plan for and use food in your kitchen

Reports estimate that over 500 million tons of household food went to waste in 2022–enough to end hunger in regions like Sub-Saharan Africa, roughly 15% of the world's population. This wasted food is in addition to food lost in the supply chain between harvesting and retail. As with other waste ideas discussed here, the first step to reducing food waste is to avoid overbuying and to work to use up the food you have on hand. Raise your hand if you've had leftovers from dinner, packaged them away in a container to store in the fridge, and then thrown them away days later. Unfortunately, I'd guess we've all been there.

Meal planning a straightforward way to reduce overbuying. On Sundays, my friend Amy makes a menu for the upcoming week. She takes inventory of what she has on hand and plans meals using those ingredients. She makes a short list of things she may need and shops strictly from that list at the supermarket. If she ends up with leftovers, she tries her best to use them for later meals, be it lunches or dinners, or sometimes even breakfast. Occasionally, she will need to get creative to reuse the food, but she tries to reduce what goes into the trash. Leftover rice and veggies? Mix up a quick vegetable fried rice with a few supplements. Zest lemon and orange peels from other recipes (or from snacks) and freeze for future use. Make cold brew from coffee grounds or use it as plant fertilizer. Old (but not moldy) bread is perfect for croutons or bread pudding! You can even save the peels from cutting onions, carrots, celery, and garlic to make a yummy vegetable stock. Use that stock to add more flavor to soups, stews, rice, and quinoa.

Trigger: *You bought a rotisserie chicken and ate most of the meat for dinner. You have some leftover pieces of meat plus the carcass.*

Routine: *Freeze the carcass to make chicken stock later. Shred the meat for chicken tacos tomorrow night.*

Reward: *Future delicious meals, less waste, and money saved.*

Bonus Advice: You can find many ideas for turning leftovers into new meals online–search "reusing leftovers."

Idea: Freeze perishables and take out what you need when you need it

Extend the shelf life of perishables like bread, fruits and vegetables, meat, and even dairy products by storing them in the freezer. Whenever you need something, take out the exact amount you plan to use. Freezer storage ensures nothing goes to waste and helps keep groceries fresh for longer. This habit reduces the frequency of shopping trips, making life a bit more convenient and efficient. You can do the same with foods with a longer shelf life too. Buy pasta, rice, and beans in larger quantities (which also reduces packaging) and store them in jars or other smaller containers in your pantry for daily use.

Trigger: You took the kids to the U-Pick Farm and brought home an excessive number of fresh strawberries.

Routine: Vacuum pack or package the berries in freezer safe containers and store them in the freezer.

Reward: Berries when you need them and reduced waste from spoiled berries you couldn't use before they went bad.

Idea: Rinse and reuse product containers for different purposes

Look at the products you bring home, and you'll see many of them come in containers ripe for reuse. Pasta sauce jars, sandwich meat boxes, and mixed nuts containers are prime for reuse. Today my fridge holds chopped carrot sticks stored in a glass jar that previously held marinated artichokes. Leftover cooked spaghetti noodles are sitting in a plastic deli meat box. Keeping these containers is also fantastic for sending leftover food with family and friends–there's no need to worry about getting your container back. They can reuse or recycle it at home.

Trigger: You finish a prescription medication and the pharmacy's amber bottle is not recyclable in your area.

Routine: Wash the bottle and use it to store your phone charger for travel. (Another idea is to check whether your pharmacy will accept returned bottles; some will.)

Reward: An untangled cord in an organized carry on. (Or no bottle to dispose of if the pharmacy takes it.)

Idea: Consume less paper and use the paper you have as many times as you can

Recall, the top goal for waste is not to create it. Consider whether you need a hard copy before hitting the print button or writing something down on a notepad. Print only what's necessary and access the rest electronically. If you must print, use the duplex function on the printer to print on both sides of the page, ideally using recycled paper.

Collect paper printed or written on only one side instead of adding it straight to the recycling bin. If the content is not sensitive, turn it into scratch paper for jotting down notes and ideas or doing quick calculations (I do this a lot!). Give it to your kids to draw on. Cut it down and use a binder clip or staple to make a mini notepad (we have several of these too!). When they were younger, my kids routinely came home with flyers and notices from school that I reused in my printer. It didn't matter if there was already something printed on the back of the page when I printed things like draft versions of this book for editing, for example.

If you're writing something temporarily, say notes or brainstorming in a meeting, use a dry erase board or electronic document instead of paper flip charts. Take a picture of the board to save the information before erasing it.

Trigger: You printed a document and realized it contained incorrect information afterwards.

Routine: Save the misprints in a special location near the printer to access when you don't need a pristine printout.

Reward: Clean paper next time you need to print something for reference.

Sustainable Swaps to prevent or reduce waste

- I'd be remiss if this list didn't include swapping a paper coffee cup with your reusable mug or a plastic shopping bag with a reusable one.
- Swap your baby's disposable diapers for cloth. Cloth diapers are reusable, while disposable diapers can take hundreds of years to decompose. Manufacturers often use natural materials to make cloth diapers as well.
- Swap out paper towels and plastic-based sponges with cloth cleaning rags made from old t-shirts or towels
- Use a washcloth in the shower instead of a nylon plastic loofah. Washcloths last much longer than loofahs, and they need fewer resources to be produced.

- Use laundry detergent sheets instead of liquid or powdered detergent. Sheets often come in plastic-free packaging versus liquid detergents in plastic bottles. They also use non-toxic, biodegradable ingredients.
- Compost your waste when possible instead of tossing it in the trash bin. You can then fertilize your garden with the compost when it's ready.

Additional resources for ecohabit and sustainable swap ideas

Books

365 Ways to Save the Planet: A Day-by-day Guide to Sustainable Living by Georgina Wilson-Powell - A year of daily tips for sustainable living.

Go Gently: Actionable Steps to Nurture Yourself and the Planet by Bonnie Wright - Learn about environmental topics, examine your home for improvement areas, track behaviors, and watch buying habits.

Green Living Made Easy: 101 Eco Tips, Hacks and Recipes to Save Time and Money by Nancy Birtwhistle - Tips for living an eco-friendlier life without sacrificing comfort.

Lagniappe Leftovers by Susanne Duplantis - Recipes for reusing Southern Louisiana leftovers.

Social Media

The following accounts are on Instagram but may also be available on other platforms.

@livekindly - Sustainability news and tips

@nancy.birtwhistle - Innovative ideas and timesaving swaps to make as little an impact on the environment as possible

@nasaclimatechange - Information and data about our global climate

@one5c - Meaningful changes everyday people can make to help combat the climate emergency

Websites

Australian Department of Climate Change, Energy, the Environment and Water - Ideas to reduce waste.
https://www.energy.gov.au/households/reducing-waste

US EPA - Tips for reducing water use.
https://www.epa.gov/watersense

US EPA - Tips for becoming more energy efficient.
https://www.epa.gov/energy/reduce-environmental-impact-your-energy-use

US National Park Service - "Leave No Trace" seven principles to protect nature while spending time outdoors.
https://www.nps.gov/articles/leave-no-trace-seven-principles.htm

CHAPTER 7

Anticipate and Overcome Obstacles

> The block of granite which was an obstacle in the pathway of the weak, becomes a stepping-stone in the pathway of the strong.
>
> – THOMAS CARLYLE

As with most things, creating new habits won't always run smoothly. You will hit snags. You'll be outside your typical environment, where you've set up triggers and helpful resources. Or maybe you'll lack the confidence to exercise your habit in public. You'll make excuses for why you can't. Now what? Be prepared for it!

As you lay out your new ecohabit, take time to envision obstacles and plan for them. Will resources not be available? Will people get in the way? Will your old habits tempt you? Put together a list of situations and obstacles you may encounter using your *Preparing for Obstacles* worksheet. Classify them by how likely they may happen. Then, focus on the higher priority obstacles as you figure out how to deal with each one. Treat each obstacle as an opportunity to solve problems.

You can call these solutions your Plan Bs or contingency plans. These plans will outline what you need to do if an expected situation doesn't materialize. A typical way to plan contingencies is using an *if, then* method. This method is effective because you write your plans in a language your brain easily understands. Say your goal is to reduce vehicle emissions. Your ecohabit is to bike to work every day instead of driving. One morning you are feeling tired and don't want to bike. You could force yourself to bike, but you should also have a Plan B. It could be: "If I feel too tired to bike to work, then I will call a friend to carpool or take public transport instead of generating air pollution from my solo ride in the car." Whatever your Plan B is, it needs to be something that works for you, tailored to your behavior and what you have available.

Here's a situation I ran into that attempted to foil my recycling goals. The kids and I ate lunch at a fast-food restaurant one afternoon. My food came in a paper bag, and the kids' meals were in cardboard boxes. We ate at the restaurant, immediately taking our food out of the bag and boxes, so there was no time for them to get greasy. (Honestly, we didn't even need the bag and boxes. Avoiding unnecessary packaging should have been the restaurant's first step.) We finished with clean, perfectly recyclable containers, but the restaurant didn't have recycling facilities. Rather than toss the bag and boxes into the waste bins with the ketchupy wrappers, I brought them home and put them in our curbside recycling bin. I overcame the obstacle of a lack of recycling facilities and successfully contributed to reaching my North Star of recycling paper and cardboard waste. My Plan B was: "If the places I go do not have recycling facilities, I will take the recyclables home." Maybe doing this would have embarrassed you (my kids were embarrassed)–that's OK! Figure out a Plan B that works for you.

Be creative and think broadly when contingency planning and harness the power of *if, then*. Put your ideas down on your *Preparing for Obstacles* worksheet. Choose the ones you want to focus on and that will be most impactful. Write these down on your *Planning My New Ecohabit* worksheet in *if, then* format. Maybe you'll eventually run into obstacles you never thought about. Challenge yourself in those situations to support growing your ecohabit rather than giving up. Practice makes progress!

> **My Plan B:**
>
> If I'm out and buy a canned drink, then I will take the can home to recycle instead of throwing it in a trash can.

Besides planning for obstacles, you will also need to figure out what it means to be successful. How will you know when you've established a new ecohabit? What will be your marker of success? How will you celebrate success?

Reflect

What's one obstacle that has derailed your eco-habits in the past, and what 'if, then' Plan B could you create right now to handle it differently next time? What's your plan for when life gets busy or chaotic? How will you keep sustainability on your radar?

Chapter Takeaways

Envision and plan for obstacles as you lay out your new ecohabit.

Your Plan Bs will outline what you need to do if an expected situation doesn't materialize or if something unexpected turns up.

Harness the power of if, then when crafting your Plan Bs.

Do what works for you! Progress, not perfection.

CHAPTER 8

Define Success

> If one advances confidently in the direction of his dreams, and endeavors to live the life which he has imagined, he will meet with a success unexpected in common hours.
>
> – HENRY DAVID THOREAU

You have your goals set, your plans in place, and your potential obstacles figured out. You're almost ready to go with your new behaviors. How will you know when you've been successful in establishing your new ecohabit? If it's not obvious, how will you measure success? What signs will show you that you've accomplished your goal?

I spoke earlier about having a firm understanding of where you're starting from–a baseline. Do you always leave the water running while brushing your teeth? Do you drive to work every day? Does all your waste go to the landfill? Knowing where you're starting from is key to knowing if you've made it to your destination. Each of your goals and routines should have specific success markers. Define these markers as objectively as possible, so you don't have any wiggle room to say you've reached your North Star when you haven't. The markers should be visible and easy to track.

If you're trying to reduce water consumption, review your last few bills and see how much water you ordinarily use or the average charge. Then, set a volumetric or dollar reduction target. You can track your efforts by seeing how much your usage or bill decreases month to month. You'll know you've been successful at building your new habit when you see the use decrease and ultimately reach your target. Alternatively, there are apps you can download onto your phone to track and measure water and energy use.

Say your North Star is to reduce gasoline use in your car by taking public transport three days a week. You'll need to know how much gas you buy on average before you build your habit. Then you can check your fueling frequency to observe how it's changing once you take public transport. Another way to track this is if you use a credit card, where you can track your purchases. Understand all the factors associated with your success marker and choose one that isn't influenced by too many things. Your commute's gasoline consumption may go down, but your driving may increase on the weekends, taking up the savings.

In my recycling example, I didn't know specifically how much trash or recycling we generated before starting our recycling habit (I should have done a waste audit!). But I knew that most weeks we partially filled one recycle bin and filled a trash can to the top. Now we have three recycling bins, two of which are full most weeks, and the trash can contains only one or two bags of refuse inside. While I can't confirm quantitatively whether my family has successfully built a habit, I can qualitatively say we have a strong recycling habit at our house.

Don't underestimate the *feeling of* success as a marker, either. Research shows people are unlikely to attempt new behaviors unless they are confident their actions will have a meaningful impact. Satisfaction with new habits ranks high and affects whether you stay consistent.

> **My Success Markers:**
>
> At least two full recycling bins each week
> Reduced amount of waste in the general trash bin

Over time, as we work to avoid waste generation, I might have to update my metric of two full recycling bins down to one full recycling bin. Your *Planning My New Ecohabit* worksheet has a place to write a few success markers for your North Star.

You've completed your planning steps–now it's time to practice your new habit!

Reflect

How could you measure progress in your sustainability journey, and what milestones matter most to you? What's one habit you've built that felt successful? What made it work? How can you apply that insight to building ecohabits?

Chapter Takeaways

Understanding your baseline–or starting point–is a key point of comparison as you work through building a new ecohabit.

You need to name clear success markers before building your new habit, so you can easily tell when you've reached your North Star.

Don't influence your success markers with too many variables or craft them to be easy to wiggle out of.

Don't underestimate the feeling of success as a marker.

CHAPTER 9

Get Going!

The secret of getting ahead is getting started.

– UNKNOWN

It's GO TIME! You don't need a special time or place to build your eco-friendly habit, so jump in. Once you start, be sure to track your progress so you can see how you're doing along the way. Research has shown that emotions create habits, so not only should you track your progress, but you should celebrate each step along the way to stay motivated.

Check your progress

Journals or worksheets can help with keeping track of how you're doing. Seeing progress with my own eyes is essential to keep me motivated. Relying only on my brain to monitor how I'm doing as I build a new habit is a recipe for disaster. A tracker lets me note down highlights or struggles I've experienced along the way. If I had an aha moment, where I realized something worked well or didn't work at all, I note it down for future reference.

Tracking can sometimes feel like a burden on top of building a new habit, but once the new habit has become second nature, you won't need to track anymore.

Many generic habit tracker apps are available today if using your phone works best for you. Some people create bullet journal trackers, and others use ready-made trackers in their planner system. Or make up your own–you know what works for you. Harness that energy! Whatever tool you decide on, don't overcomplicate it or spend more time tracking your habit than working on it. Take a few minutes a day to reflect and write down how your efforts at change are going.

Pay attention to these daily check-ins and what they're telling you, then use them in a weekly review to reflect on the past few days and to look forward to the next. Do you see patterns developing? Do you have proper reminders and systems in place for success next week? Use your observations to make tweaks to your triggers, environment, or Plan B. Do you have a weak link in the habit chain? The more you understand your patterns, the better you can adjust and change bring you closer to your North Star. Daily and weekly reviews shouldn't be burdensome or complicated. Taking a few minutes to think ahead and plan will set you up for success. If you need a tool to keep track, try the *Progress Check* worksheets to help you complete your daily and weekly reviews and track your progress.

What were my big successes?

Did I run into obstacles?

What could I have done better or differently?

What could help make doing my new habit easier?

Harness the power of 90 days

I'm sure you've heard it takes 21 days to form a habit. Unfortunately, that's not true. It's not 30 days or 45 days either. Since various factors influence creating a habit, there's no one length of time for it to take. The behavior you're trying to cultivate, the circumstances you're in, and the number of times you perform the routine all play into how long it may take. One study showed that on average it takes about two months for a new behavior to become automatic–and that's if you're doing it every day. The study participants took from 18 to 254 days to form a new habit. Building a new habit may take you anywhere from two to eight months.

Work on building your ecohabit for 90 days. Ninety days will give you time to make the routine a habit, sort out any bugs, and then embed the ecohabit deeply into your lifestyle.

Stay motivated

You'll find your initial energy and early achievements will get you going, but as you improve by exercising your new behavior, it may be harder to tell if you're making progress. Don't let this derail you. Messing up once or twice won't stop your long-term progress. **Give yourself grace for the times you get off track and don't beat yourself up.** Things will happen! You're human. If you're moving in the right direction, stop judging yourself and view any missteps as learning opportunities. Figure out what would make you successful the next time the situation comes up and plan to do it. Don't be slow to get back on track. Sometimes it may be necessary to remind yourself of your North Star. Check whether you are focusing on the outcome instead of the process and be sure you're thinking back to your Why to keep your motivation up. People change by feeling good, not by feeling bad–so learn from your mistakes and move on.

Recognize you will have an identity shift as you work through this change. Your brain (and possibly other people) will tell you that you can't do it, or it won't stick. **Embrace your new identity as someone who wants to change help the environment.** You <u>can</u> change! Say it aloud to remind yourself if you need to (go ahead, do it now!): I CAN CHANGE!

Here are a few affirmations you can say (aloud or in your head) to counteract the negative voices.
- I can follow through with this.
- I can change.
- I'm the kind of person who recycles.
- I'm the kind of person who conserves energy.

Tailor an affirmation to your North Star or to the identity you'd like to have for yourself. **Immerse yourself in your new identity.** Go to events that bring together people, products, and services to help you grow. Find a community that understands the journey you're on. A group of people to whom you can ask questions, find innovative ideas to try, celebrate new achievements, and commiserate if things are going the way you planned. The library and community center are excellent resources; they might direct you to recycling or zero waste groups in your area. Ask your local bulk store or sustainable product shop if they know about any local groups. Facebook, meetup.com, and nextdoor.com are popular places to find groups interested in living sustainably.

While online, find the experts and follow their social media pages. James Clear (@jamesclear), the author of *Atomic Habits*, is on my follow list, as is Keep Louisiana Beautiful (@keeplouisianabeautiful) to learn about making my community cleaner and greener. Browse hashtags like #eco-friendly, #sustainablefashion, #reducewaste, or #climateaction to find the latest content. Watch YouTube to educate yourself. Learn the terms and tools you need to be familiar with and use them. Do you know the difference between biodegradable and compostable? What do greenwashing and fair trade mean? Don't forget to update your profiles to announce your new identity. Do it at a pace and in a way that reflects you and your personality.

When I started writing this book, it felt like a project or a hobby. I didn't consider myself a writer. But I realized that because I am writing, I am a writer! I updated my Instagram and Facebook profiles to include writer as one of my descriptors. I followed other writers, built relationships with them, and learned from them. I told my colleagues at work I am a writer and described what I am working on. I've even attended writers' conferences to learn the ins and outs and terminology. Immersing myself in the writing community gave me confidence as a writer.

Be positive about your change and think optimistically about your efforts–recognize how far you've come

> My Motivator:
>
> There's no reason to trash aluminum. Do the right thing.

instead of focusing on how far to go. Visualize yourself successfully carrying out your new habit. Or even better, visualize what Earth looks like for your future great-great-grandkids because of your improved behavior. Explore ways to elevate your mind and motivation each day. You could read about influential people you admire or find a recent social media post from someone successful at making changes like yours. Remember: it will take time to build change–change in yourself and change in the world. The longer you work at building or revising a habit, the more automated it will become. Note down on your *Planning My New Ecohabit* worksheet one thing you can do to keep motivated when progress seems slow.

Admittedly, sometimes it just helps to have someone else on board during the journey. Doing new things alone can be hard without a support system in place. Enlist a friend or loved one to partner with you in your change. **Surround yourself with like-minded people who can help you when you need motivation or encounter a new challenge.** Talk with others and tell them how well you've been doing building your ecohabit. They will ask you how it's going, supporting you when you need it most, and holding you accountable. My friend Cindy and I never miss the opportunity to share what we're doing around sustainability when we catch up. Whether it's new behaviors, ideas, or books we're reading, there's always something to inspire us.

Having someone else around will give you space to vent and figure out how to simplify things and celebrate progress, even if it's only with a little happy dance. If you feel alone during the process, you'll lose momentum. Jot down a few names of people who will support you on your *Planning My New Ecohabit* worksheet.

> **My Support Group:**
>
> My family and friends who recycle

Reflect

When progress feels slow, what helps you stay committed to your goals? What visual or emotional cues remind you that your actions matter? Could you create more of them?

Chapter Takeaways

Don't overcomplicate checking your new habit's progress; don't spend more time tracking the habit than building it.

A few minutes a day plus a weekly reflection are enough.

Use these reviews to find emerging patterns, ensure you have the right triggers in place, and check whether your environment is supportive for nurturing your new eco-habit.

Give yourself 90 days of effort. Building a new habit takes time, and 90 days will give you time to sort out any bugs and embed the new behavior into your lifestyle.

Give yourself grace when you stumble. You're human!

Embrace your new identity as someone who does what your habit is looking to achieve and immerse yourself in that identity.

Be positive and think optimistically about the change you're making.

Surround yourself with like-minded people who can help you when you need a boost.

CHAPTER 10

Break Bad Habits

> The greatest discovery of my generation is that a human being can alter his life by altering his attitudes of mind.
>
> – WILLIAM JAMES

People form bad habits because they have short-term benefits, and unfortunately, we often ignore the long-term consequences. What can you do about habits that are harmful to the environment? It's possible to break unfriendly habits, but it may take time. Unfriendly habits are still habits with a trigger, a routine, and a reward. The secret to breaking a bad habit is to stop the ability to complete the habit and replace it with a new one. You do this either by keeping the same trigger-routine-reward but changing the tool associated with the habit, as discussed in *Chapter 5: Put Your Eco-habit Together*, or by swapping out one of the trigger-routine-reward components to change the habit.

Another way to change an unfriendly habit is to make it harder to complete by breaking part of the habit chain. Usually, changing only one aspect of the habit suffices to break it. First, you'll need to understand the unfriendly habit's trigger, routine, and reward. Check out the *Breaking Unfriendly Habits* worksheet to identify the parts and assess which bit you can change to redesign it into something better. Many times, a new routine will be the most effective way, but changing the trigger can also work.

After deciding which part of the habit you want to update, you'll need to think about what the replacement could be to make the habit more environmentally friendly. Turn to the *Rebuilding Unfriendly Habits* worksheet and jot down ideas for replacing the part of the habit you want to change. Use the insights you gained with your *Breaking Unfriendly Habits* worksheet. Here's an example of how to change the routine.

One habit many of us have is drying everything in the dryer once it's washed. You open the washer and drag everything into the dryer that's right next to it. The screen tells you the estimated drying time. Bed comforters, blankets, bathmats, and towels have a longer dry time than anything else. To save energy used by the dryer, you could dry them on a line outside during the summer months. To change the routine of this habit, take everything to the clothesline outside instead of tossing it to the dryer. The trigger is the same (washing is done). By changing the routine, you also inherently changed the reward. Before, the reward was clean, warm towels and blankets. Now the reward is a bit of Vitamin D from the sun while hanging up the washing, the fresh smell of linens dried on the clothesline, and the warm feeling in your heart from using natural, renewable energy to dry these heavy items.

Here's another example where the routine stays the same, but the tools changed. A pet peeve of mine is using paper plates routinely for meals at home. Sure, paper plates may be convenient, but they use resources to produce and get and take up limited space in our landfills after a single use. Reusable plates also take resources to produce, obtain, and wash, but you can wash them with the pots and pans used to make meals. Making it harder to use paper plates is simple: stop buying them. If the plates aren't available, you'll have to go with a reusable dish. This example has a part two, however: washing the dishes so you can have clean ones available. We are all busy, but it's not difficult or time consuming to scrub and quickly rinse lightly soiled dishes and save the dirtiest dishes for the automatic dishwasher. I set up a drying station next to my kitchen sink for just this purpose.

Once you have your unfriendly habit rebuilt, revisit Chapters 4 through 9 and build a new habit to make sure this changed habit sticks. Keep in mind, your old habits never go away. They will always hide in the shadows of your brain, ready to come back. It's like how you never forget how to ride a bike or roller skate–things you may have learned as a kid. That's why it's so important to focus on replacing the bad habit with a new one versus trying to suppress it entirely with self-control. Self-control is a limited resource! Like muscle strength, at some point, willpower runs out.

You can't depend on your willpower alone to break bad habits. The more self-control you exert throughout the day, the less you have as the day goes on. You may not notice it, but all the decisions you make throughout the day burn a little willpower. The traffic is thick, and you try to stay calm. You come home exhausted, and the family is hungry, so you push through it to make dinner. All these instances take up willpower. If you're depending on willpower to suppress the old, bad habit that rears its head at the end of the day, you likely won't have any left to give.

A deep motivation to change and understanding this driver is also critical to breaking bad habits, maybe even more so than creating new ones. Since you'll have to work against your brain and the old habit, you'll need to make hard decisions sometimes. A firm belief in yourself, knowing you can make this change, is the secret to success. Remind yourself throughout the process of why you're breaking the bad habit. Remind yourself why you set this North Star. Breaking an unfriendly habit may take longer than creating a new habit, so don't let this discourage you if it happens.

Dig deep into understanding the triggers and rewards to come up with a game plan. It may sound simple to change a bad habit, but it takes effort, self-awareness, and motivation to turn things around. Smaller changes can make transforming an unfriendly habit more bearable. Remember, we are all different, and we all progress at different rates.

Reflect

What's a small, sustainable change you could make to your environment that would disrupt an old habit loop? How could you make a new routine more appealing or rewarding than an old one? If you could design a "habit swap" plan for the next week, what old routine would you replace—and with what?

Chapter Takeaways

Bad habits are still habits made up of a trigger, a routine, and a reward.

The secret to breaking a bad habit is to take away the ability to complete the habit or replace it with a new habit.

Changing one aspect of a bad habit suffices to break it, but you'll need to understand the anatomy of the bad habit first.

Many times, changing the bad habit's routine will be the most effective method, but changing the trigger can also be helpful.

Old habits never fully go away, so replacing them with a new habit can be more helpful than trying to suppress the old bad habit.

A powerful motivation to change and understanding the bad habit's driver are critical to breaking bad habits.

PART THREE

Increase Your Impact

Congratulations! Now that living sustainably is becoming second nature, it's not time to stop. It's time to push your ecohabit-building skills harder. You might be wondering what you can do next to broaden your positive impact on the world. This part will help you to:
- Cultivate your ecohabits by expanding them so they have a wider impact on new topics or locations.
- Inspire others to build their own ecohabits to broaden your environmental impact outside of your inner circle.
- Advocate for and invest in change

CHAPTER 11

Cultivate Your Ecohabits

> Do what you can, with what you've got, where you are.
>
> – SQUIRE BILL WIDENER

You started small by building or changing one habit to get the hang of things. Studies have shown that people like to be consistent–so if you have one ecohabit going strong, you're more likely to be successful at making other positive changes to your lifestyle. The company IKEA launched a program to study the sustainability journey of a group of its customers. They found that when people in the group made one change–such as reducing food waste–they often also moved on to make other beneficial changes, like energy conservation.

One possibility for expanding your ecohabit is to build upon the changes you've already made. For instance, if you're now successfully recycling all aluminum cans that come into your home, you can try adding paper, cardboard, or glass to the materials you recycle. Say you've built an ecohabit to limit the amount of water you use while bathing. The next step could be to build a new ecohabit that helps you limit the amount of energy you use in your home.

Another way to grow your new ecohabit is to expand *where* you do it. You can continue to recycle aluminum cans at home, but consider broadening your aspiration to include recycling aluminum cans at work or school as well.

My family has recycled at home for years. When my husband started a new job and routinely saw bottles and cans in the trash at work, he asked if he could start a recycling program. After gaining support, he bought bins for the shared areas in each building at their worksite. The company already had a contract for metals recycling in place since he worked at a light industrial facility, so the aluminum cans went out with the industrial recycling. He expanded his recycling habit from home to work.

As you plan to make these changes, be sure to revisit your Why and your North Star. Do they hold true for the new habit? If not, take time to find your new Why to make sure your motivations align with your behaviors. Next, review your plan for the first habit change and figure out what may need tweaks for you to be successful at cultivating the habit. Will your same kitchen recycle bin work if you plan to add paper to the mix? If not, decide how to redesign your environment to increase the ability to recycle paper. Go back to your *Planning My New Ecohabit* worksheet to help plan out your growing habit and ensure you have enough time, motivation, and ability to be successful.

Reflect

What's a natural next step for an ecohabit you might already have? Can you build on what's already working? What's one barrier you've overcome in your current sustainability journey and how can that experience help you tackle bigger challenges now? What would it look like to turn an ecohabit into a lifestyle, not just a task?

Chapter Takeaways

Cultivate your ecohabit by building on the foundational change you've already made.

Try adding similar activities to the ecohabit you've already built.

Expand your ecohabit to other locations if you've focused on building it in one only place.

Review your existing ecohabit plans to decide whether they'll hold true for expansion and tweak them as necessary to stay successful.

CHAPTER 12

Inspire Others to Do Better

> Plant trees for the future, not for today.
>
> – UNKNOWN

People will watch you on your path to building ecohabits. That alone makes you an inspiration! When they continually see you reducing water use or buying items with minimized packaging, they may ask questions and want to do the same. Those around you may feel the same way you did before you began your journey to save the planet: wanting to make a change, but unsure where to begin or what to do. Teach them your skills to help make their desired changes. Guide them from watching to doing. In *Tiny Habits*, B.J. Fogg describes two ways to create culture change: by sharing and by doing.

Share your story

Sharing your story is an easy way to help others start their journey towards protecting the environment. Talk to them about what you've been doing and the changes you've noticed so far. Help them visualize what the world could look like in the future if change doesn't start now. Describe your Why or reasons for making a change. Share insights from your journey, including any lessons you learned or things that were most helpful. Leverage your social media platforms. If you decide to take this approach, be sure to do it constructively—no guilt trips or reprimands, no trying to force them to change too.

Have conversations with whoever will ask questions and actively listen to your change story. Behavior change conversations must grow organically out of relationships and interactions to take root and to be meaningful. Preaching or engaging superficially will doom you to failure. You could create support networks by organizing a group around sustainable living or building ecohabits. Resource groups like this are an efficient way to engage people to change their behavior and to help one another along the way. Invite experts who can advise and help everyone achieve their goals.

Do it together

You're already setting an example for others through your growing ecohabits, so why don't you ask them to come along and do it with you? If they're interested, teach them what you've learned about why Earth needs change and how to go about it—share your enthusiasm. Find new ecohabits to build and do it together. And don't forget to celebrate their successes! Not sure who to help? Start a new tradition around sustainable living.

Teach your family about overconsumption and excess waste. Explain to your kids why you're making the decisions you are, whether it's buying in bulk or walking to the store versus driving. Help them understand the benefits of recycling, waste and water minimization, and energy efficiency. Include them in the decisions you're making for your household. Focus your conversations on the process of change rather than the outcome. These types of discussions reinforce the value of creating sustainable change whose byproduct is the desired longer-term result. The key is to allow them to adapt to change at their own pace. It takes time for people to adjust to new scenarios, so be respectful that they may not get on board as quickly as you did.

Invite your friends to the farmer's market to buy fruits and veggies produced closer to home, which likely will have reduced transportation and packing impacts than those bought in a traditional grocery store. Be sure to encourage your partners in change along the way! When you build an environmentally friendly culture in your circle, it will expand. The small decisions we make compound and make a bigger difference in the world. Remember, every bit adds up.

Reflect

What's one sustainable habit you practice that others have noticed or asked about? How did that feel? How do you share your environmental values? Through words, actions, or creative expression? How do you balance sharing your habits with respecting others' pace and perspective?

Chapter Takeaways

You're an inspiration to others just by starting. They may not tell you, but they are watching what you do with curiosity.

Inspire others to start their change journey by sharing your story—share insights from what you've learned or how you've overcome challenges.

Focus conversations on the process of change rather than the outcome.

Ask them to join you! Find a common ecohabit you'd like to work on building together and get started.

CHAPTER 13

Move Outside of Your Inner Circle

> You cannot hope to build a better world without improving the individuals. To that end each of us must work for his own improvement, and at the same time share a general responsibility for all humanity, our particular duty being to aid those to whom we think we can be most useful.
>
> – MARIE CURIE

So far, I've limited the examples for broadening your ecohabit's to those around you, who you know personally. But what about everyone else? What about the neighbor a few blocks away whom you've never met? What about the stranger in the grocery store? How can you help them make positive changes when you don't even know them?

Advocate for change

As you make your journey towards creating new habits to live sustainably, you may notice certain resources aren't as readily available to you as you thought they might be. Curbside recycling or community composting may not be available where you live. Not having certain services available will affect your ability to build selected habits. Your favorite takeout restaurant uses Styrofoam containers or automatically gives out straws with every drink. Do you give up then? What can you do?

Tell your local government's Department of Environmental Affairs (or similar office) that there's a desire for services currently missing from your community. Outline other things that need changing to help the environment. Rally like-minded friends and neighbors and encourage them to advocate too. The voices are louder, and those with influence may hear the messages better when groups put pressure on making change. I read a story about a bag ban in one city. A group of citizens decided they didn't want plastic grocery bags at their supermarkets any longer. They pressured the local grocery stores to forgo the bags; a few stores voluntarily agreed to take part in the bag ban. Now, both businesses and citizens were calling the city to get rid of the bags. The city council passed a bag ban, forcing all grocery stores to eliminate plastic bags. The ban pressured the customers to use their own bags.

If you read or hear about policies or legislation under development, support them by attending public consultation meetings and giving your input. When environmental issues show up on the ballot, promote community awareness of the topic. Talk to your neighbors and coworkers about the proposals and vote for them.

Spark change locally by recommending environmental improvement projects. Do public buildings and other places encourage your community to act sustainably? Do they offer opportunities to recycle or reduce waste or energy use? If not, talk to the organization or department in charge about making a change. When they were little, my kids played sports year-round at the local public playground. What comes with outdoor sports during hot southern summers? Plastic drink bottles and aluminum cans! Every summer during baseball season, the trash cans were overflowing, primarily with plastic water and sports drink bottles. I spoke to our local Department of Environmental Affairs about why the playgrounds didn't have recycling stations, since we had a curbside recycling program for our homes. The same garbage trucks picked up at our houses and the playground, so why couldn't the same recycling trucks pick up? Their response: our community hadn't built a recycling culture, so people probably wouldn't use them. If you still don't see the change you want to take place, volunteer in your community to help improve its environmental consciousness.

Host a clean-up. It could be a small group (like my daughter and I were on Earth Day), or it could be a larger, formally organized event. Every fall, a local conservation group in my area hosts a Beach Sweep. They invite the entire community to gather along the shore of Lake Pontchartrain to collect trash and debris. The organization provides gloves, bags, and extra supplies to help with the collection. One year the sweep picked up over 58,000 pounds of trash. Picking up the trash beautifies the lake area, but it also helps maintain the efficiency of the drainage system and the lake's water quality.

Another way to kick off a culture change in your community is to give a talk at a school or the library. I especially like giving talks to kids because they usually ask a lot of questions and are eager to learn new things. When my son was learning about oil spill response in fifth grade, I asked the teacher if I could come to class to speak. He was ecstatic to give me class time to educate the students about how oil spills can impact the environment and what we can do to prevent spills or to clean them up if they occur. On another occasion, I spoke about recycling, waste minimization, and reusable products with my daughter's kindergarten class. That was a fun one! I brought props with me, and the kids loved passing around cans from my recycle bin, reusable lunch bags, and compostable sandwich bags. I even showed an age-appropriate video about how waste gets from your house to the landfill and what happens to it then.

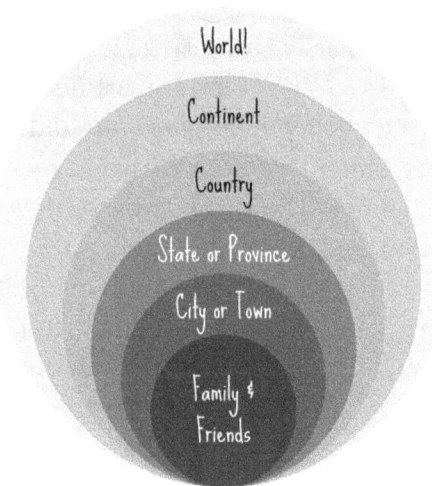

Invest in change

Besides voting on or advocating for environmental issues that matter to you, put your dollars to work. Spend your money where you want to see change happen or to support ongoing efforts. Invest in companies and businesses whose sustainability ideals and strategies align with your environmental goals. Many funds are investing in alternative energies such as solar and wind to replace the fossil fuels responsible for climate change.

Purchase products from certified B-corps. B Corporations are businesses that meet the highest standards of verified social and environmental performance, public transparency, and legal accountability. Shop at local stores specializing in sustainability. My town has a zero waste supply and bulk refill store that also offers plastic-free, eco-friendly products. Not sure if you have a similar shop in your area? Do an internet search with keywords like *sustainable store, bulk supply store, or zero waste store* plus your city or town name.

Various organizations actively focus on protecting the environment and fighting climate change. Nonprofits tend to operate on slim budgets and appreciate any financial help they can get. Donate to these organizations to help fund projects to protect the planet. If possible, find and support a charity or non-governmental organization doing this sort of work in your community. Well-funded organizations include The Nature Conservancy and the Natural Resources Defense Council, so research smaller agencies to help them amplify their work. To find a recipient, decide what topic you'd like to impact and in what region, for instance, coastal erosion on the US Gulf Coast. You can use sites like Charity Navigator and GuideStar to find nonprofits and assess their backgrounds to figure out which will receive your cash. A quick search for *coastal erosion Louisiana* on both sites returned 15 results for me to assess.

Most credit cards nowadays come with some sort of rewards program. You can earn anything from cash back, to magazines, airline miles, or hotel room nights. Rather than spend your annual cash back reward, use it for the donation mentioned above; it doesn't impact your budget since it's "free money" from the credit card. Hand over your airline miles so organizations can travel to conduct field research or make trips to lobby for policies or to take part in rallies. Donating miles allows them to spend their money on things besides travel expenses. Some credit cards automatically give a percentage of every purchase to environmental organizations. Check out the terms, conditions, and rates to make sure the card works with your budget and lifestyle.

Invest in local programs like community solar panels, where you can receive renewable energy or financial benefits. One such program is Michigan Solar Communities. Subscribers to the Community Shared Solar program earn credit on their electric bills based on the energy produced by their designated solar panels (not by the amount of energy the subscriber uses). These panels are part of a community array rather than being installed at the subscriber's home.

Reflect

How could you involve others in your habit-building to multiply impact? If you had the time, energy, or resources, how would you expand your sustainability efforts? How could you identify the ripple effects of your ecohabit on your mindset, your environment, or others around you?

Chapter Takeaways

Advocate for change outside of your inner circle by rallying your community to campaign for missing services in your area or to recommend environmental improvement projects to your local government and businesses.

Attend public consultation meetings to give input supporting emerging policies or legislation in your area.

Get outside and host a clean-up or give a talk at a school or library.

Put your dollars to work and invest in companies and products that produce results.

Donating to organizations focused on protecting the environment and fighting climate change.

CHAPTER 14

Enjoy the Results of Your Hard Work

> We cannot live only for ourselves. A thousand fibers connect us with our fellow men; and among those fibers, as sympathetic threads, our actions run as causes, and they come back to us as effects.
>
> – HENRY MELVILL (modernized)

Remember the introduction when I told you that you can change the world? I said you can make your eco-friendly changes stick. Think about how you feel about those statements now. You might have felt skeptical back on page one. I hope you feel capable now. I hope you feel empowered; you are ready to make sustainable changes. Your ecohabits combined together with the actions of others make a difference for the health of our planet.

I wrote *Second Nature* is to shine a light on how we can apply our knowledge about habits to help improve our environment. You have the knowledge to help the environment. Everything you need is in this book. You picked it up because you want a better world in the future. You took the step to learn. You must build your first ecohabit for your contribution to count. Others will benefit from your consistent actions, and you will benefit from theirs.

And that's the point, isn't it?

Maintain your progress to see long term results. Use the steps you learned here to stay on track.

- Set reminders to review your progress and celebrate your wins.
- Focus on one ecohabit at a time. Don't try to change everything at once. Master one before you move on to the next.
- Find a partner. Share your goals with a friend or family member. You will stay motivated when you work together.
- Keep this book nearby. Read specific chapters again if you feel you need a refresh.

Building lasting change is not a race. It's not a competition. It's part of the bigger picture. Do what you can with what you have and what you hope to accomplish. Don't sit back and do nothing.

You have the tools. You have the knowledge. Your actions today determine the health of the world tomorrow. Don't wait for a "perfect" moment. Pick one habit; master it; then pick another. Live your life as if the future depends on you. It does.

Start now.

APPENDIX 1

Habit Building Worksheets

Here's a look at the worksheets I've referenced throughout the book. As a bonus, you can **download** them for free to print out and use to build your ecohabits! Find them at https://oxfordcommapress.com/worksheets.

Planning My New Ecohabit

My North Star

This is important to me because...

My new Routine

| The Trigger | The Reward |

Resources I need:
-
-
-
-
-
-

Obstacles & how I'll overcome them:
-
-
-
-
-

What does success look like to me?

Who can motivate me?

To motivate myself I will...

Put this where you can reference it often!

Preparing for Obstacles

Use this worksheet to brainstorm different situations and obstacles that might prevent you from successfully completing your ecohabit. Rank their likelihood to occur and then write down possible solutions to overcome them. Focus on addressing high-ranking obstacles.

Situations & Obstacles	Likelihood to occur	Possible Paths to success
	High / Medium / Low	
	High / Medium / Low	
	High / Medium / Low	
	High / Medium / Low	
	High / Medium / Low	
	High / Medium / Low	
	High / Medium / Low	

Weekly Progress Check

Week of:

My North Star

Reflections from the week   How did the week go? How do I feel about my progress? Did I notice any patterns emerging?

Adjustments I can make   Are the trigger & reward working for me? Are my Plan Bs sufficient? Is my environment set up in a supportive way? Do I need more or other resources?

My plan for next week   What are my focus areas to work on? What changes will I put into place & test out to help me to be more successful?

Put this where you can see it and check in weekly!

Daily Progress Check

Week of:

My North Star

Successes	**Opportunities**
What am I glad I did/didn't do? What went well?	What do I wish I had/hadn't done or done better?

MONDAY

TUESDAY

WEDNESDAY

THURSDAY

FRIDAY

SATURDAY

SUNDAY

Put this where you can see it and check in daily!

Breaking Unfriendly Habits

My Unfriendly Routine

I want to change this habit because...

Answer the following questions to help identify the parts of your unfriendly habit. When you're done breaking it down, you can use the next worksheet to rebuild it into a new ecohabit!

Identify the Trigger

Where were you?
What were doing doing?
Who else was there?
What time of day was it?
What did you do right before?
How were you feeling?

Will changing any of these things help you to do better? Write your possible triggers in this box.

Identify the Reward

What urge were you satisfying by completing this routine?

How did you feel after completing the routine?

What did you gain from completing the routine?

Write your possible rewards in this box.

What can you change or design out of the Routine or the Trigger? Focus on changing only one! Use the following worksheet to help lay out a new ecohabit.

Rebuilding Unfriendly Habits

Describe your unfriendly habit using the anatomy you identified using the previous worksheet. Tick the box of the part you want to change.

The Trigger	The Routine	The Reward
☐	☐	

Jot down ideas of how to change the selected part of your habit.

Select your change and write down your new ecohabit.

The Trigger	The Routine	The Reward

Go back to the Preparing for Obstacles & Progress Check worksheets to plan out and track your new ecohabit!

APPENDIX 2

Other Ways to Live More Sustainably

You've likely recognized other ways to improve your environmental footprint that don't involve the basics of a trigger-routine-reward ecohabit. Read on for some tips to help you make more mindful shopping choices.

More sustainable swap ideas

Manufacturers design many products today for convenience rather than longevity. Single use products are prevalent in both the health and beauty and cleaning aisles. A few years ago, I tested sustainable alternatives to products I was using. I found some keepers and tossed a few into the figurative recycling bin. Here are a few swaps I tried and some things I routinely use instead of the single use or throwaway version.

Use	Unsustainable Product	Sustainable Swap
Bathroom	Feminine hygiene pads and tampons	Washable period panties and washable flannel pads (made by me from scrap fabric)
Bathroom	Plastic throwaway razors	Stainless steel metal razor with recyclable replacement safety blades
Bathroom	Single use cotton face pads and cotton balls	Flannel washable face pads (made by me from scrap fabric)
Bathroom	Facial tissue	Flannel handkerchief (made by me from remnant fabric)
Cleaning	Sponge or pad mop	Washable fabric mop heads
Cleaning	Chemical fabric softener	Wool dryer balls
Cleaning	Window cleaner	Vinegar and water mixture
Cleaning	Plastic sponges and scrubbers	Ribbed cotton washable dishcloths
Cleaning	Paper towels	Cotton washable kitchen towels and cleaning cloths
Kitchen	Plastic cling film	Beeswax wrap and silicone covers
Kitchen	Plastic zip top bags	Silicone zip top bags and compostable paper sandwich bags
Kitchen	Paper coffee filters	Mesh metal reusable coffee filter

Consider whether you need to purchase an item before you buy it

People have also written article upon article about the mental and emotional aspects of retail therapy. But sometimes things don't need to be purchased, particularly if they end up discarded before too long. Say no to unnecessary or impulse purchases, even if buying them makes you feel good. Find other ways to get your fix, also known as the reward part of a habit. Last weekend, I realized I had reward credits built up at my favorite clothing store. A sale email hit my inbox (trigger). I filled up my online cart—more than the value of my reward (routine). My soon-to-be purchases excited me (reward). Before I completed my order, I moved on to something else and told myself I'd come back and consider how I felt about my shopping spree later. Today, I cleared out my cart and closed the tab in my browser. I didn't need any of that stuff. Taking a pause can break the trigger-routine-reward cycle.

Find what you already have that will fill the need before going shopping

Sometimes you must purchase an item. Before hopping in the car or online, figure out if you already have a solution that would work in place of what you're considering buying. A while back, I'd been seeing recipes for Starbucks copycat egg bites. I love those and always need a quick and easy breakfast to heat in the morning before I sit down at my desk to work. The recipes I found said to use a silicone egg bite mold. I don't have one, but I wanted to make egg bites one Sunday. Before giving up, I thought about what I had on hand that I could use instead. I remembered I have quite a few silicone muffin cups. I use them for muffins (of course), to separate food in lunch boxes (bento style), to hold small things during crafts, etc. So, I made egg bites in my muffin cups. They weren't as smooth or as pretty as Starbucks', but do you know what? They all went down the same and were delicious without buying a new gadget.

Shop pre-owned

Give new life to something already out in the world and don't introduce a new one into the cycle. Websites such as eBay and Facebook Marketplace have become popular through the years as people declutter their homes of things they no longer need. Mercari, Poshmark, and DePop are fun places to buy or sell clothing and other items online. I've sold baby clothes and furniture, old lawnmowers and tools, clothes I have outgrown, books, and more. I've also picked up quite a few deals: my daughter's beloved, like new, pink high top Converse sneakers, soccer cleats for my son, new-with-tags shorts for myself, and even my husband's truck.

The adage "Your trash may be someone else's treasure" didn't come into play for no reason. Yard sales, flea markets, swap meets, and thrift shops are all wonderful places to find what you're looking for or to unload something you no longer need. Your donations to charity may reduce your tax liability too. It may take you longer to find or unload something, but it goes a long way knowing someone in need will love and use it again. Things to consider buying used:

- Clothing for the whole family (make it fun and have a swap party with your friends)
- Books, DVDs, video games, and consoles (organize a game trading party with your kids' friends who have the same consoles and are bored with their old collection)
- Furniture
- Appliances and electronics, including cell phones
- Baby gear (though make sure it's safe and not expired or recalled)
- Handbags and luggage
- Cars and other vehicles
- Tools
- Sports equipment
- The list is endless!

Borrow instead of buying

Borrow or rent things instead of buying them if you won't use them frequently. You can rent things like tools, vehicles, DVDs and games, clothing, and even sports equipment. Borrow a formal dress or tuxedo from a friend who wears your size instead of buying a new one. Pick up your next bestselling book at the public library or from your local Little Free Library.

Be a conscious consumer when you need to buy new

Success across all aspects of our lives depends on considering sustainability when making purchases. Sustainable or earth-friendly alternatives to typical things are showing up on the market. Finding them might take a little effort and buying them might mean a little more money in the short term. If you decide to search for these types of products, follow these six tips to help you find sustainable products that fit your needs.

Step 1: Focus on a product type

Is it skincare or trash bags? Clothing or kitchen tools? What are you shopping for? Focus on one product type at a time so you don't get overwhelmed.

Step 2: Figure out which of that product's qualities matters most to you.

Let's take toothpaste. Do you want it triclosan free? Do you want it made with natural materials? Does it need to be free of outside packaging? Or should it be free from packaging altogether to create zero waste (are you willing to make it yourself)?

Ask these fundamental questions to narrow down your personal decisions. These may not apply to you, but consider:
- Is it sustainable?
- Is it ethical?
- Is it organic or natural?

- Is it locally sourced?
- Does the manufacturer give back to environmental or humanitarian causes?

Step 3: Do some online research

Using your answers to these questions, search the internet for products that may meet your criteria.

Step 4: Review the ingredients list and packaging

Once you've narrowed down your options to a few that fit your needs and values, closely examine what they're made from. Sometimes advertising is misleading, and products may have other additives or materials.

Step 5: Before you buy, quickly research the company

Is the company donating to causes you support? Is it certified as environmentally or socially responsible by a reputable agency? Is it meeting the criteria you defined in Step 2? If so, then....

Step 6: Buy it!

Figure out if you can source it locally before ordering online. While doing your research before buying, it may also be helpful to visit local stores to find the brands and options available near you. You might have a gem sitting right in your neighborhood that could save you time and shipping emissions.

References

Introduction

UN Environment Programme. "Facts about the Nature Crisis." United Nations, April 28, 2025. https://www.unep.org/facts-about-nature-crisis.

The Coca-Cola Company. "Coca-Cola Collaborates with Tech Partners to Create Bottle Prototype Made from 100% Plant-Based Sources," October 21, 2021. https://www.coca-colacompany.com/news/100-percent-plant-based-plastic-bottle.

Chapter 1

The Times Picayune Editorial Board. "The Water Is Nice, but Lake Pontchartrain Is Risky for Swimmers: Editorial." NOLA.com, July 24, 2015. https://www.nola.com/news/politics/article_b6e4b949-e942-5062-9961-c67e9446c7d3.html.

U.S. Geological Survey. "How Much Water Is There on Earth?," November 13, 2019. https://www.usgs.gov/special-topic/water-science-school/science/how-much-water-there-earth.

Petruzzello, Melissa. "Water Scarcity." In *Encyclopædia Britannica*, September 5, 2025. https://www.britannica.com/topic/water-scarcity.

UN-Water. "Water Scarcity." United Nations, 2021. https://www.unwater.org/water-facts/water-scarcity.

Meeting Coverage and Press Releases. "Stressing Risk of More Suffering, Death, Speakers Say Financing, Infrastructure, Policy Changes Crucial to End Global Water Crisis, as Conference Concludes." United Nations, March 24, 2023. https://press.un.org/en/2023/envdev2057.doc.htm.

BBC News. "What Is Climate Change? A Really Simple Guide." July 30, 2025. https://www.bbc.com/news/science-environment-24021772.

The World Bank. "Trends in Solid Waste Management," n.d. https://datatopics.worldbank.org/what-a-waste/trends_in_solid_waste_management.html.

Locker, Melissa. "This Bootcamp Turns Kids into Plastic-Fighting Superheroes." Most Creative People. Fast Company, May 23, 2018. https://www.fastcompany.com/40576787/this-bootcamp-turns-kids-into-plastic-fighting-superheroes.

"Food Waste FAQs." U.S. Department of Agriculture, n.d. https://www.usda.gov/foodwaste/faqs.

Chapter 2

Sörqvist, Patrik, and Linda Langeborg. "Why People Harm the Environment Although They Try to Treat It Well: An Evolutionary-Cognitive Perspective on Climate Compensation." *Frontiers in Psychology* 10, no. 348 (March 4, 2019). https://doi.org/10.3389/fpsyg.2019.00348.

Vinokor, Rory. "Why Don't We All Go Green?" Environmental Leadership, Action and Ethics. Columbia University, April 2, 2014. https://edblogs.columbia.edu/scppx3335-001-2014-1/2014/04/02/why-dont-we-all-go-green.

Hall, Michael P., Neil A. Lewis, and Phoebe C. Ellsworth. "Believing in Climate Change, but Not Behaving Sustainably: Evidence from a One-Year Longitudinal Study." *Journal of Environmental*

Psychology 56 (April 2018): 55–62. https://doi.org/10.1016/j.jenvp.2018.03.001.

Orion, Nir. "An Earth Systems Curriculum Development Model." In *Global Science Literacy. Science & Technology Education Library*, edited by V.J. Mayer, 15:159–68. Dordrecht: Springer, 2002. https://doi.org/10.1007/978-1-4020-5818-9_11.

White, Katherine, David Hardisty, and Rishad Habib. "The Elusive Green Consumer." *Harvard Business Review*, July 1, 2019. https://hbr.org/2019/07/the-elusive-green-consumer.

Eckhardt, Giana M., Russell Belk, and Timothy M. Devinney. "Why Don't Consumers Consume Ethically?" *Journal of Consumer Behaviour* 9, no. 6 (November 25, 2010): 426–36. https://doi.org/10.1002/cb.332.

Thøgersen, John. "A Cognitive Dissonance Interpretation of Consistencies and Inconsistencies in Environmentally Responsible Behavior." *Journal of Environmental Psychology* 24, no. 1 (March 2004): 93–103. https://doi.org/10.1016/s0272-4944(03)00039-2.

Chapter 3

Markman, Arthur B. *Smart Change: Five Tools to Create New and Sustainable Habits in Yourself and Others*. New York: Penguin Group, 2014.

Geng, Liuna, Xiao Cheng, Zhuxuan Tang, Kexin Zhou, and Lijuan Ye. "Can Previous Pro-Environmental Behaviours Influence Subsequent Environmental Behaviours? The Licensing Effect of Pro-Environmental Behaviours." *Journal of Pacific Rim Psychology* 10 (January 1, 2016): 1–9. https://doi.org/10.1017/prp.2016.6.

Chapter 6

US Geological Survey. "Water Q&A: How Much Water Do I Use at Home Each Day?" Water Science School, June 20, 2019.

https://www.usgs.gov/special-topics/water-science-school/science/water-qa-how-much-water-do-i-use-home-each-day.

US EPA. "Fix a Leak Week," February 3, 2017. https://www.epa.gov/watersense/fix-leak-week.

Water Footprint Calculator. "Saving Water in the Shower and Bathtub," August 2, 2017. https://www.watercalculator.org/posts/shower-bath/.

US EPA. "Bathroom Faucets," October 20, 2016. https://www.epa.gov/watersense/bathroom-faucets.

U.S. Energy Information Administration. "Gasoline Explained," June 9, 2022. https://www.eia.gov/energyexplained/gasoline/use-of-gasoline.php.

World Wildlife Fund. "Save Energy by Adjusting Your Thermostat." 2013. https://www.worldwildlife.org/magazine/issues/winter-2013/articles/save-energy-by-adjusting-your-thermostat.

Direct Energy. "How to Lower Your Electric Bill by Adjusting Your Thermostat," April 17, 2018. https://www.directenergy.com/en/learn/reduce-energy-costs/how-much-can-you-save-by-adjusting-your-thermostat.

Scorzafava, Lauren. "Light Is Energy: Estimating the Impact of Light Pollution on Climate Change." DarkSky International, August 2, 2022. https://darksky.org/news/light-is-energy-estimating-the-impact-of-light-pollution-on-climate-change.

Tide. "Washing in Cold Water." Accessed January 6, 2023. https://tide.com/en-us/our-commitment/turn-to-cold.

Ocean Conservancy. "Splash: 2024 Report," August 1, 2025. https://oceanconservancy.org/wp-content/uploads/2025/08/Splash-2025-Spring.pdf.

UN Environment Programme. "Food Waste Index Report 2024. Think Eat Save: Tracking Progress to Halve Global Food Waste," March 2024. https://doi.org/978-92-807-4139-1.

Chapter 8
Dean, Jeremy. *Making Habits, Breaking Habits: How to Make Changes That Stick*. Richmond: Oneworld, 2013.

Chapter 9
Fogg, B.J. *Tiny Habits: The Small Changes That Change Everything*. S.L.: Houghton Mifflin Harcourt, 2019.

Lally, Phillippa, Cornelia H. M. van Jaarsveld, Henry W. W. Potts, and Jane Wardle. "How Are Habits Formed: Modelling Habit Formation in the Real World." *European Journal of Social Psychology* 40, no. 6 (July 16, 2010): 998–1009. https://doi.org/10.1002/ejsp.674.

Chapter 11
Ellsmoor, James. "77% of People Want to Learn How to Live More Sustainably." *Forbes*. Accessed December 16, 2020. https://www.forbes.com/sites/jamesellsmoor/2019/07/23/77-of-people-want-to-learn-how-to-live-more-sustainably.

Chapter 13
Kellogg, Kathryn. *101 Ways to Go Zero Waste*. New York, NY: The Countryman Press, A Division of W. W. Norton & Company, Inc, 2019.

WDSU. "2019 Beach Sweep," September 16, 2019. https://www.wdsu.com/article/2019-beach-sweep/29073344.

Department of Environment, Great Lakes, and Energy. "MI Solar Communities." State of Michigan, 2024. https://www.michigan.gov/egle/about/organization/materials-management/energy/renewable-energy/mi-solar-communities.

Chapter 14

Mind Body Green. "6 Simple Ways to Be a More Conscious Shopper." Accessed August 24, 2018. https://www.mindbodygreen.com/0-24010/6-simple-ways-to-be-a-more-conscious-shopper.html.

Author's Note

We've done some hard work to help save the environment. Let's get out there and enjoy it! Go hiking, walking, swimming, running, or biking–do anything to get outside! Get some exercise and enjoy nature. Take advantage of the calm and focus that spending time with nature provides.

Use the hashtag #SNecohabits on Instagram and Facebook. Share a photo of your first ecohabit in action or post your biggest challenge and success story to connect with others on the same journey. Give that hashtag a follow too. Improving our planet's health is a community effort; let's help each other out!

I sincerely hope you enjoyed *Second Nature*, and it's helping you set off on a refreshed journey of change and improvement. Please leave a review where you bought it or on Goodreads. Reviews help others to discover and take advantage of the advice I've shared. Thank you!

I'd love to hear from you!

- Lori@oxfordcommapress.com
- https://www.linkedin.com/in/LoriDowns
- https://www.instagram.com/LoriDownsWriter
- https://www.facebook.com/LoriDownsWriter

Acknowledgments

I can't write acknowledgments without thanking my family, Corey, Caleb, and Sarah, for believing that I could write this book and encouraging me to do so. Thank you for going along with all the new ecohabits I've tested (even the harebrained ones) and for providing the words on the tip of my tongue that I couldn't produce when needed.

Thanks to my parents, Roy and Marty, for tirelessly listening to me go on about recycling and waste minimization and talking about climate change. Thank you for the support you give me no matter what!

Big hugs go to Ian, my boss when I came up with the idea for this book. I think at one point you were almost more excited about me writing it than I was! Thank you to my beta readers Arnold, Bram, Julie, Matt, Sam, Vishwa, and Mike. Your eagle eyes, constructive criticism, and additional ecohabit suggestions made *Second Nature* a better book.

Kudos also go to the Jefferson Parish Public Library for supplying quiet writing spots, interlibrary loans, free Wi-Fi, and stacks of inspiration surrounding me as I wrote. Borrowing books from the library is my favorite ecohabit.

To my friends, colleagues, and social media followers who helped me toe the line by asking me how the book was coming: I hated telling you I had made no progress. Thanks for keeping me accountable.

And finally, to everyone who cares about improving our earth for future generations: even if this book encouraged you to build only one new ecohabit, I've accomplished what I set out to do. Thank you for reading and thank you for creating change.

ABOUT THE AUTHOR

Lori Downs is an environmental engineer and recognized climate and sustainability leader with over 25 years of global experience. She has chemical engineering degrees from Tulane University and the University of Notre Dame and has empowered thousands of individuals globally to adopt environmentally friendly behaviors that have resulted in significant and lasting change.

Lori encapsulates her extensive expertise in her debut book, *Second Nature*. She believes that changing habits, whether in a global corporation or a household, takes time and persistence but is essential for lasting cultural change.

She lives in the Greater New Orleans area with her family, where she champions ecohabits at home, such as meal planning to reduce food waste and using reusable products. However, she is still trying to get her kids to turn off the lights when they leave the room.

www.ingramcontent.com/pod-product-compliance
Lightning Source LLC
LaVergne TN
LVHW010219070526
838199LV00062B/4655